Ri

THE
NET EFFECT

RANDOM HOUSE
BUSINESS BOOKS

© Richard Lord 2000
All rights reserved

Richard Lord has asserted his rights under the Copyright, Designs
and Patents Act, 1988, to be identified as the author of this work.

First published in 2000 by Random House Business Books,
Random House, 20 Vauxhall Bridge Road, London SW1V 2SA

Random House Australia (Pty) Limited
20 Alfred Street, Milsons Point,
Sydney, New South Wales 2061, Australia

Random House New Zealand Limited
18 Poland Road, Glenfield,
Auckland 10, New Zealand

Random House (Pty) Limited
Endulini, 5a Jubilee Road, Parktown 2193, South Africa

The Random House Group Limited Reg. No. 954009

Papers used by Random House are natural, recyclable products
made from wood grown in sustainable forests. The manufacturing processes
conform to the environmental regulations of the country of origin.

ISBN 0 7126 6974 4

Companies, institutions and other organizations wishing to make
bulk purchases of books published by Random House should
contact their local bookstore or Random House direct:
Special Sales Director
Random House, 20 Vauxhall Bridge Road, London SW1V 2SA
Tel 020 7840 8470   Fax 020 7828 6681

---

www.randomhouse.co.uk
businessbooks@randomhouse.co.uk

Typeset in Baskerville & Gill Sans by
MATS, Southend-on-Sea, Essex
Printed and bound in Great Britain by
Biddles Ltd, Guildford and King's Lynn

To Kath

CONTENTS

Introduction   ix

1. Some good news   1

2. Customers   60

3. Staff   96

4. Money   135

5. Marketing   152

6. Competitors, suppliers and partners   206

7. Conclusion   222

INTRODUCTION

You'll have heard a lot about the internet, I would imagine, and how it affects business. But if you work in a real business, most of it will have seemed pretty much irrelevant to what you do. First there was all that stuff about how it'll put you out of business within the next twenty minutes unless you appoint a collection of 23-year-olds to run it, raise £100 million, waste it all on ill-targeted advertising and start direct-selling paperclips online. Then, a few months later, you'll have read that the internet is in fact rubbish after all, that anyone who has anything to do with it will never make a profit, and that they'll all go bust by next Wednesday.

My advice would be to ignore most of it. Concentrate on what matters to you, and to your business. Understand that the real inheritors of the internet won't be the millions of wet-behind-the-ears companies that are springing up like mushrooms. Some will be successful. But in any new economy, a million companies are founded, and only a few stand the test of time; a combination of failure and acquisition will consolidate every internet market until only the strongest survive.

That doesn't mean that the internet isn't a valid business tool. It's the most exciting thing to happen to businesses in decades. And chief among the inheritors

THE NET EFFECT

of its glorious legacy will be companies with meaningful, established businesses.

The internet is changing everything, but above all, in the midst of all the sound and fury it is vital not to panic. Be calm. Make yourself a cup of tea. Lie down. Think very carefully. Lots of new things are happening, and many of them will affect the way you operate as a business, or as a business person. The important thing is to identify which are important, which affect you personally, and how you need to change to accommodate them. That's why I've written this book: to help you to get a sense of perspective and identify what's really important.

The internet has always been about explosions. It was built in case they happened. In 1969, the US Government, twitchy about the possibility of nuclear attack, decided to safeguard its military systems by building, as an experiment, an alternative communications network based on phone lines. It was called the ARPANET. The military, and the academics involved with the project, thought 'Hey! This is a pretty neat way for us to communicate' and decided to carry on using it. It was flexible, easy to use and, best of all, it allowed lots of people to talk to each other and share information. They didn't realize it at the time, but the internet had been born.

Thirty years later, and that tiny branch of the military-industrial complex has become the most important cultural phenomenon of the age. But the important thing to bear in mind is that it is still in essence exactly what it was then: a super-duper, high-octane communications network, a collection of wires and widgets that let people talk to each other. That's the heart and soul of the internet, and that's what makes it interesting. It caught on because it allowed everyone in the world to talk to everyone else in the world relatively cheaply and very conveniently. Suddenly, interacting with other human beings, wherever they might be, became as simple as switching on a computer.

But it wasn't just a case of businesses tuning in to something buzzy and exploiting it commercially. It's more fundamental than that. The internet is having a more profound effect on business than any development since the Industrial Revolution precisely because it's all about communication. It is, variously, a new marketing medium, a new sales channel, a new tool for customer service, a new way of streamlining business relationships, and a new way of communicating with each individual customer. It's all those things and more: it gets to the heart of a business, fundamentally affecting what it does and what it is. The internet is making companies re-engineer the way they do things. It introduces new efficiencies into the way they trade. It opens up opportunities for new companies. It shakes industries up from head to toe. And so, over the following chapters, I'm going to talk about a group of companies that have been facing up to the challenges of the internet and getting to grips with how it changes what they do.

Raw materials are the traditional building blocks of any economy. But in the so-called information age, less tangible resources become equally, if not more, important. No one controls computing power, for example; it's not a scarce commodity. No one owns it, and so anyone can exploit it. If you offer a service on the internet, there's nothing to stop anyone else offering exactly the same service. So the emphasis shifts to a company's relationships with its customers. The person who consumes the product or service that company supplies is suddenly at the centre of everything. How companies treat their customers, how they interact with them, develop their relationships with them and extract long-term value from them is at the heart of everything; it's a new economics based on consumption, rather than on production. Understanding that is a big part of what will separate the winners from the losers.

This is an era of mass customization, with the internet at its heart. Long ago businesses served their small number of customers on an individual basis. But the Industrial Revolution ushered in an era when companies were able to trade on a massive scale, whilst mass production appeared to herald the end of personalized service. In fact, it had simply gone into hiding, and it took the internet to bring it back to life. Suddenly, businesses could trade on a massive scale, but at the same time treat each customer as an individual. So an online shop can learn from what people have bought in the past, offer them relevant products, build up a profile of their behaviour, target promotions to them as individuals, and get to know them far better than any high-street shop, even one they use every week – while still shifting millions of units to millions of people.

Business is about communication. Companies do business by communicating with each other, and they transact with consumers by selling to them at places where they communicate. Where people communicate, there's money to be made. The internet is a re-inventor of business, rather than just another channel for it, precisely because at its heart it's a communications medium – the best one ever. It existed for over two decades before anyone other than hardware and software manufacturers worked out how to make it pay. The turning point was the invention, in the early 1990s, of the world wide web. The web turned the internet from being a largely text-based techie toy into something with sound and pictures which anyone could easily turn on and use. Commercial concerns stepped up their interest. Just a few years later, they've taken control.

Thirty-plus years after the ARPANET came into being, nuclear armageddon still hasn't materialized. But the internet fizzled away with its own series of minor explosions, each in its own way remarkable, and with a cumulative effect far beyond anything anyone could have predicted. The internet has carpet-bombed the collective mentality to such an extent that it has become an absolutely central part of our culture. The internet is everywhere. Well over half of all Americans, and more than 40 per cent of people in the UK, have access to it in some form. And while the commercial explosion of the medium has been brewing for a while, it's only in the last couple of years, with the mass adoption of the web, that it has reached critical mass. In the UK, really massive consumer take-up of the internet was kick-started with the debut in late 1999 of the subscription-free internet service providers, the best-known being Freeserve. Since then, the price of access has steadily dropped, and consumers have flooded onto the internet in their droves. That, more than anything else, forced business to sit up and take notice. The flood of consumers onto the net was followed by a huge surge of business interest.

Not only were established businesses cottoning on to the possibilities; all sorts of new ones began to spring up. It was an explosion of entrepreneurial activity the UK had never seen before. The opportunity to launch new and interesting businesses meant that starting up a new company was suddenly something anyone could do. Lots of companies with .com at the end of their names came into being, each with a clever idea exploiting the special qualities of the internet. Suddenly, all sorts of people had ideas for companies, and found that they were able to get funding to launch them, and launch them quickly.

The most potent symbol of that movement is First Tuesday. It is, depending on your perspective, either the digital world's most exciting networking event or a financial cattle market full of clueless youths with ill thought-out business plans scribbled on the back of a cigarette packet. It started as a small, informal meeting of a few people who had ideas for internet companies with the one or two venture capitalists brave enough to invest in that kind of company at the time. It has become a phenomenon. Thousands of people attend the events, and they take place in eighty-five cities around the world. Most of the attendees are budding entrepreneurs with ideas that they hope will make them the next millionaire whizz-kid. Everyone in the internet industry has an idea for a start-up; the internet economy has become the sexy place to work, and talent is flowing into it.

Established businesses now have to sit up and take notice. They know that everyone in business needs to think about the internet. The majority of UK businesses are doing so, but a lot of them are doing it for defensive reasons. If they want to compete with nimble-footed start-ups, they need to actively engage with the internet. A breed of new companies, together with some ambitious and far-sighted established ones, have done strange things with the business rulebook. They may not have rewritten it – a lot of what they've done has been grounded in traditional business practice – but they have added quite a few appendices.

There is suddenly a huge thirst for knowledge, and for people who possess it. With barely a single exception, when I ask the bosses of British internet companies what the single biggest thing holding back their business is, they unhesitatingly reply 'recruitment'. There is a massive skills shortage, a shortage of intellectual capital, and a desire to meet and share information. It's ironic that for this, the most information-rich medium in history, the business surrounding it suffers from a chronic shortage of real knowledge.

For the last three and a half years, I've been working for *Revolution*, the UK's leading magazine about business in the digital economy. The changes I've seen during that period have been phenomenal. The internet has gone from being a fringe activity to a central part of our culture. And my friends and family have started to say things like 'Looks like you might have been right about all this internet stuff', which, if nothing else, is a great relief.

The job titles of the people I speak to as an internet business journalist have changed dramatically. Two or three years ago it was junior marketing execs; some far-sighted companies might have had an internet manager. Now it's all CEOs and managing directors. They're the ones who have to understand how the internet will affect their business, because it affects it from top to bottom. It has gone from being the preserve of techies, through being a useful place where companies could promote their products and services, to in many cases *becoming* those products and services. It is fundamentally integrated into business.

Three years ago, the amount of business being transacted online in the UK was negligible. Those of us writing about it got terribly excited about amazon.com going public in the States. We wrote a story if anyone launched an e-commerce site. The phrase 'passing fad' was thrown at me with alarming regularity, and the bosses of big corporations scoffed at the idea that this plaything of geeky computer types would ever have any sort of meaningful effect on their business.

One of the most startling developments over the last year is the amount of mainstream media coverage the internet now gets as a business medium. My magazine used to operate in more or less virgin territory. Now the big business weeklies are full of it, the TV is full of it, and camera crews crawl round industry events looking for sexy entrepreneurs to interview. The internet receives saturation media coverage, and amazingly, it's the business people who are the subjects. In early 2000, you couldn't move without falling over an article about Martha Lane Fox of lastminute.com, so much so that it started to get boring.

But amid all the talk of 22-year-olds who have made their first billion in six months and gone public with a company which is now worth more than Texaco, it's easy to forget that for most people, and for most companies, the internet isn't about that. More simply, it's about understanding how the goalposts have been shifted.

The internet moves at an insane speed. Everything changes every couple of months. It's not unusual for internet companies to more than double in size every year. Trading conditions change, the competition changes, customers change – everything is in a constant state of flux. People talk about web years; like dog years, there are about seven of them to every calendar year.

It makes writing a book like this an interesting experience. Books take a long time to write, and so I'm writing a lot of it three web years or more before it gets published. In other words, everything will almost certainly have changed beyond recognition by the time you read this. That's why I've tried to avoid staring into my crystal ball too often.

As I said earlier, I'm aware that you will already have heard how the internet will re-invent business as we know it. Less clear is what it all really means, and what each individual business should be doing in the light of the internet, beyond getting scared and hiding under the boardroom table or hoping it'll go away before you retire.

The internet is doing things to business, it is seen as a threat. The way internet companies – particularly the technology suppliers – market themselves to prospective clients often fits into the 'miss out on this and you'll be lying in the gutter drinking meths in two years' time' category. What I hope to do over the following chapters is to show you that the internet is also doing things *for* business, and try to explain how it can help companies, how it can make organizations successful, and how they need to evolve to take advantage of it. I'm going to do this by looking at how certain companies have faced the challenges thrown up by the internet and tried to make it work for them.

It isn't just about the internet any more; it's about business. Because, if you're involved with business of any sort at this particular time, the internet fundamentally affects what you do. It might be a new channel to promote your services, it might be a way to communicate with suppliers and customers, or it might be the whole basis of what your company does. The point is that intelligent, strategic thinking about the effects of digital media is no longer an option for business people. It's a necessity. You might decide it's not for you, and that *is* still an option – just. But you should at least be thinking about it now, rather than later. Because if you don't think about ways in which you can bite big chunks out of your own business, well, you can rest assured that the competition – whether your traditional competitors, or companies you haven't even heard of yet – will be thinking about it very hard indeed.

CHAPTER ONE

SOME GOOD NEWS

It's extremely difficult for established companies to compete on the internet. I admit that on the face of it that doesn't sound like good news. But there are some very good examples of traditional companies that are triumphing online, despite all the disadvantages they apparently labour under.

More than anything else, the biggest problem facing established businesses as they try and engage with the internet is inertia. Many are structurally ossified; they cannot adapt fast enough to change, particularly when it happens as rapidly as it does in this new economy. The internet moves at incredible speed, with new ideas, new people and new companies constantly entering the market. The competitive landscape changes daily. There's a frantic imperative to be the first to market, to grab as many customers as quickly as possible and dominate a particular sector. That's why internet-only companies, the so-called dotcoms, have to attract so much investment: they need to move at such a speed that they simply can't afford to grow organically.

In that context, it's difficult for established

2
THE NET EFFECT

businesses to keep up. The way they raise money is rarely through massive external investment. It's rare for their internet thinking to start by considering how much money they need to get to market super-fast and dominate a sector; instead they'll think about how much budget they need to allocate to get their web presence to a certain place. The problem is that they're likely to make that calculation in much the same way as they would with any other budget. But online, they need to get further in a shorter space of time than they ever have before. That means investing a lot of money. And it's difficult for a company to reconcile sensible budgeting and financial control with chucking a load of money at something they're not sure when – or sometimes even how – they're going to make money out of. That's particularly pertinent if that company is publicly traded, and has shareholders who are naturally going to question any expenditure which appears out of proportion with the expected return on investment.

Even if an established business is bright enough to realize that it needs to approach the internet in a way it's never approached any business issue before, it may find that it is unable to. The way the company is structured may not accommodate the kind of rapid growth, the kind of seismic upheaval, or the kind of high-risk environment, that characterizes internet companies. Most companies are not set up to deal with this kind of thing. Why would they be? A company that has done more or less the same thing for years has no need of the sort of culture that will allow it to change quickly, and it's unlikely to employ the kind of people with the willingness, or the expertise, to force that kind of pace of change. If an online competitor comes along and does the same sort of thing that company does, only more efficiently, more cheaply, or simply better, that company can easily end up a supertanker trying to turn round in the middle of the English Channel: it's facing the wrong direction to start with, and there are massive practical hurdles to overcome before it can even start facing the right direction, let alone start ploughing forwards.

Brent Hoberman, co-founder of Britain's best-known home-grown internet company, lastminute.com, sums up the contrast. 'Dotcoms are very flexible,' he says. 'We can expand into different geographical territories, different products, different companies to do different things. Other companies have to justify changing like this, and doing it so rapidly. We not only don't have to justify it – it's actually expected of us. Traditional businesses are generally pretty slow-moving, and aren't in a position to change like we can.'

Then there's the headache of recruiting and keeping good people. Good internet staff are difficult to recruit. Internet-only companies are set up to get good staff by rewarding them generously, whether that be with large salaries, stock options or equity. It's much more difficult for an established company to pay the sort of money it needs to pay to attract and retain people if it doesn't pay those sorts of wages already. I'll talk about this more in Chapter 3.

An established company's greatest strength is the fact that it already does something: it has a business. But that existing business can also be a hindrance. When you do one thing well, you have a major disincentive to ditch that thing and do something else instead. Why should you jeopardize what you've done

---

3

SOME GOOD
NEWS

4
THE NET EFFECT

for years to do something new, especially something where the returns are so uncertain? Even if you know you need to change, you probably won't want to. It's not an easy one to sell to the staff of a company, the idea that everything they've laboured for and built up over years is suddenly going to be knocked down and swept away, and they're going to find themselves doing something else.

Dotcoms, on the other hand, have a blank sheet of paper on which to create their business, with no so-called legacy business getting in the way. And they are companies built, in the way no established company can be, on an innate understanding of the internet and the way it changes the tectonics of business.

Don't panic. The situation is not as alarming as you may think. All it requires is a bit of perspective. It's true that a lot of companies are threatened by the internet. It lays bare areas where they don't add value, where they're not customer-centric, where there are possible efficiencies that are not being exploited. It opens up the market for new players to do things more efficiently. It opens up new ways of doing business, new ways of understanding and interacting with customers. It changes everything.

The clever companies are the ones that have realized this, and taken steps to ensure that they're the ones who benefit from the internet. And there are some sizeable advantages that established players enjoy over their dotcom rivals when it comes to reaching the online customer. The internet is the greatest opportunity these businesses have ever had.

I'm going to look at a few examples of companies whose attempts to engage with the internet and make it work for their businesses are instructive, and whom we're going to be following throughout this book.

For some companies, the transition to a new economy business model is obvious. If you're, say, Dell, the world's biggest direct seller of computers, the decision is not a controversial one. You already sell PCs to people without the mediation of the big retail chains. Everything that you do offline you can do online, more efficiently and cheaply. You can give customers the chance to configure a computer to their own requirements online, without someone on the phone having to run through a list of options for monitor, printer, modem, storage, memory and so on. The buyer is presented with the information and can decide what they want in their own time. Transferring a large part of that business online is a sensible, pragmatic decision.

That doesn't make it a trivial one. Changing your main distribution channel will occasion huge organizational upheaval. A company has to rip out its own core and replace it with something different. The effect on staff is profound, of which more later. Just because a company's existing business model fits the internet reasonably well, that doesn't mean it can just turn its business around overnight and transform itself into a shiny new net company by an act of will. And it doesn't mean it shouldn't be congratulated for doing so successfully. There are numerous other direct sellers of PCs, but Dell is the one that grasped the internet nettle early and exploited the potential of the medium best.

Dell took its decision at a very early stage. The impact of the internet on business was only just

5

SOME GOOD
NEWS

6
THE NET EFFECT

starting to be felt when the company identified the medium as its key distribution channel for the future. For this it has been rewarded with a big stack of cash – at the time of writing, it was selling about $40m of computers and associated equipment off its web sites every day. In Europe, the figure is $6m a day. The internet accounts for 45 per cent of Dell's global sales.

Chris Hall, the company's internet business manager, is the man who runs Dell's internet-related operations in the UK. He's been involved in managing the company's internet strategy for a long time, and insists that the reason for its success online is that the decision was taken at an early stage, at the very highest level, and with an absolute clarity of purpose. 'Our internet business grew from a major strategic initiative globally,' he says. 'We had some very major objectives with really tight timescales. In terms of the money to fund it – well, it was just found. A unit was formed, and a guy was appointed in the US with global responsibility. We were told from the top just to make it happen. This all happened about five years ago, and its full ramifications were felt in Europe about a year later.'

Dell has the internet pegged as the future of its business as well. It is the medium that will help the company expand its reach into new territories. Dell has eighteen offices and five call centres in Europe alone, but it's looking to grow that. It is planning to launch web sites in countries where it has no physical presence – no offices, no call centres, no factories.

Perhaps one day the company will become an entirely virtual operation, but only when and where it's relevant and economically sensible for it to do so. That's not going to be the case globally for quite some time. For the time being, it manages to combine a phenomenally successful traditional direct selling business with a textbook internet operation.

There are certain products that sell well online. Steve Bennett's trick was to realize that if he was already selling one of them, then why not sell the others too. Bennett founded his first successful business, computer software and peripherals retailer Software Warehouse, in 1989. It was a big success story, growing to £100m annual revenue ten years later. The company had gone into mail order in 1992, and combined this with a network of thirty-one retail outlets.

Then everything changed. Bennett decided that the internet, the ideal direct selling medium, was the future for his company. And he decided that, while taking his existing business of selling computer software online, he would expand the range to include entertainment products like games, CDs, DVDs and videos.

The result was internet retailer jungle.com. The company was established in August 1999. Sales grew rapidly and soon overtook the combined revenues from Software Warehouse's retail and mail order operations. And so, in early 2000, the companies bowed to the inevitable and jungle.com swallowed its parent. Soon after, the decision was taken to shut down the company's retail premises and become a pure direct seller, with the internet as the primary channel. More recently, the company was bought by catalogue giant Great Universal Stores.

Bennett is frank about the reason to focus on the net. A big factor was channel conflict – it was difficult to sustain both operations side-by-side, because they had different interfaces, different ways of selling, and

SOME GOOD NEWS

frequently, different prices for the same items. 'We found that we were getting conflict on prices,' he says. 'We were selling items cheaper on jungle than in the stores or by mail order, and a lot of customers were getting confused. We needed to bring it all under the same umbrella and make it consistent. You can't sell cheaper through one medium than another if you're going to be using the same brand.

'Also, if you run a business and you own retail outlets, you have to go out and visit them, get their feedback, make sure they're happy and whatever. This is a business based on people, so I had to go and visit them. But I was spending two days of every month on the road, which was a waste of time I could have been using in a lot of better ways.

'We had to sit down and ask ourselves: is it worth us keeping retail? It was profitable, but was it where we wanted the business to be? The answer, in the long term, was no.'

This was not an easy decision. Software Warehouse's existing channels had already been very successful for Bennett, and clinging onto them, especially while they continued to make him a profit, must have been a strong temptation. It's not as if the company was struggling. In fact, Software Warehouse was the UK's fastest growing privately-owned company between 1994 and 1998, expanding at a phenomenal rate of 136 per cent a year. So abandoning the existing business and setting up as something quite different was a tremendous leap of faith.

But despite a very high cost of customer acquisition orders soared. At the time of writing the company was planning to expand across Europe, using a single centralized warehouse and a single call centre to sell across the entire continent, with local offices in each country for marketing and vendor relations. It is also looking further afield, with Australia, where Software Warehouse already has a presence, at the top of its list. And the ebullient, charismatic Bennett will probably, by the time you read this, have stamped his name across the nation's psyche in Branson-like style with a classic PR stunt: attempting to break the record for crossing the Atlantic by boat, in the company of world-famous, if accident-prone, yachtsman Tony Bullimore.

It's not just the computer and computer-related goods sectors that have seen established players, with entrenched business models, taking advantage of the opportunities the internet offers them and changing their businesses accordingly. In the travel market, for instance, easyJet has turned around everything it does to face the internet; it would be hard to find an example of an old economy company that has embraced this new way of doing business more successfully.

EasyJet sells no-frills air travel at rock-bottom prices. It has revolutionized the way short-haul flight-only travel is bought in the UK, and spawned a clutch of imitators. The company cuts out everything except the very basic business of getting people from A to B. Tickets are electronic, in-flight meals are out of the question, and travel agents are elbowed aside – all its orders have traditionally been taken by phone. EasyJet trims its prices to the bone to take account of all these savings. Margins are wafer-thin, so that at the time of writing, the company expected to make about £1.50

10
THE NET EFFECT

from each customer. Any way in which it can cut its costs is to be wholeheartedly embraced. That's why the internet was such a blessing for the company. If customers bought their flights online, there was suddenly less need for expensive call-centre staff.

The way easyJet has embraced the internet has been wholly impressive. Everything it does is designed to push people in the direction of the site. Realizing that it could cut costs by selling online, the company decided to motivate people by offering them £1 off each flight they booked that way, meaning a £2 saving on a standard return. That may not sound much, but the majority of easyJet's prices come in well under three figures, so as a percentage, and with the margins the company operates at, it's pretty generous. The company has also driven people towards its web site with newspaper promotions offering further discounted fares for buying via the web site. It also puts its flight schedules up online before it makes them available by phone; people who phone up are directed to the site.

The result is that just within two years of launching its first transactional site, the company was selling two thirds of its seats online. In keeping with its mass-market image, easyJet's parent company, easyGroup, also launched easyEverything, a chain of internet cafes. Although easyEverything is run as a separate business, the original idea was to give people without internet access the opportunity to buy online from easyJet. EasyEverything customers can visit the easyJet site for free; the rest of the time it's £1 an hour, far cheaper than rival internet cafes. So the company has gone from using the internet as a distribution channel to embracing it so evangelically that it is providing internet access. A whole slew of internet-based ventures under the easy brand have either been launched or are in the offing, covering areas such as car hire and financial services. What we have is a company which, once it saw the logic of using the internet as its main channel, has angled everything it does around the web, and turned itself into a true new-economy player.

Travel is a high information product – people need to know a lot of stuff before they buy. But with easyJet, the number of variables for a customer wanting to buy from it is relatively small: destination, time, and type of ticket. That sort of information can be conveyed far more efficiently by text on a screen than by a person using a telephone. Timetables work better online, and so do explanations of different tariffs. So, surprisingly, do destinations, particularly in the case of easyJet, whose customers don't necessarily know where they want to go. The price point the company operates at is so low that a lot of potential customers just know they want to go somewhere, for a long weekend or whatever. It's the same thought process which is supposed to inform the decision to use a web service like lastminute.com. The problem is that ringing up an airline and saying 'Hello, I want to go somewhere please' sounds a bit ridiculous; exploring the range of possible destinations on a web site is a lot easier. So as well as transferring customers from one medium to another where they're cheaper to administer, easyJet is also using the web to open itself up to new potential customers.

The opportunity was clearly there for a direct seller like easyJet to put the internet at the heart of its business. But it could just as easily not have done so.

12
THE NET EFFECT

Once again, it meant profound change within the company. And once again, it was easyJet that took the bold and imaginative leap, and has reaped the benefits. It could have been someone else – but it wasn't.

The benefits of the internet for companies whose main business involves selling products or services are fairly easy to grasp. If it's a simple product or service such as jungle.com sells, it can easily be bought online without the need for consumers to traipse around shops, so that giving them that extra choice is a sensible move. For a company like Dell, the product needs a fair bit of configuring before purchase, something that usually requires the involvement of a human being, and so the solution is to design an interface that allows customers to do that configuring themselves. For direct sellers like Dell and easyJet, the benefits are clear.

The same is resoundingly not true for a lot of other companies. There are a sizeable number which don't appear to have anything obvious to gain from the internet: it looks irrelevant to what they do. There are still more that look directly threatened by it. The internet ruthlessly exposes who adds value and who doesn't. So many companies are looking nervously at it, and wondering if they'll be overtaken by younger, leaner rivals.

It is worth looking at a few of the companies that didn't seem to have anything much to gain from the internet, to see how some visionary thinking has enabled them to embrace it, and to gain from it.

John Charcol is a company which faced up to the internet and saw it having a profound effect on the way it does business. The company is a mortgage broker. That means that it helps customers choose the best mortgage for them from a broad range of products. It traditionally does this mainly through its retail branches, and it charges a fee for doing so, typically between £300 and £500. The company is backed by Bradford & Bingley, but it's independent – its business relies on objectivity, on having a reputation for recommending the best product for each individual, irrespective of who supplies it.

The mortgage market is worth around £110 billion a year, of which around 5 per cent is arranged through brokers. The rest goes direct to the lenders or through other types of intermediary like independent financial advisers. John Charcol has about a third of the broker market, or just over 1½ per cent of the entire market. In 1999, it arranged mortgages worth £1.7 billion. The company is around five times as large as its nearest competitors.

The internet looks like a threat to a company like John Charcol. It's a medium which allows people who are looking for a mortgage, or indeed any product or service, to find out for themselves all the information they need. They can go and collect information directly from every mortgage lender, and make their own decision. Why would they pay several hundred pounds to a broker to do something that they could do for themselves? The internet looks suspiciously like the death of brokers.

John Charcol realized that people wouldn't pay for its service online, so it decided to do something pretty radical. It stopped charging for it. On its internet service, Charcol Online, launched in November 1999, the company makes its money solely from the

14
THE NET EFFECT

commissions it is paid by lenders. It was a massive cultural and business change for the company. For a start, it has cut off one of its main revenue streams. This in itself is a pretty radical move. When you add in the consideration that the fee has traditionally acted as a kind of guarantor of objectivity – we don't make all our money from commissions, so we won't just sell you the mortgage that makes us the most money – you start to realize what John Charcol surrendered when it decided to drop its fees.

Its choice was this: change what it does completely, and cut off one of its main revenue streams; or cling untenably to its existing business model. It is to the company's credit that it chose to do the former. It means it will become a more powerful player in the new economy.

Toby Strauss is managing director of Charcol Online, and the man who changed the whole nature of John Charcol's business. It was he who had to go and sell this new way of doing business to an initially very sceptical board of directors. According to Strauss, the company made a conscious decision early on that in the way it used the internet it would try to think about how it could create value, rather than how it could avoid risk. Indeed, he claims that the company goes so far as to see itself as the attacker rather than the incumbent. Rather than resting on a comfy business model and refusing to change, the company has embraced the internet in an aggressive way, using it as a way of further stealing a march on its competitors, and moving actively into new areas of business.

John Charcol has been vindicated in its approach. As of March 2000, the company did 20 per cent of its entire business online, a percentage which is increasing every month. Charcol Online turned over £35m in March, and its turnover is increasing by between 5 and 10 per cent every month. The biggest mortgage it has arranged through the site to date was worth a whopping £650,000. Strauss claims the company is on target to meet its aim of generating as much revenue online within two years as it currently does offline.

This anticipated surge in business justifies the removal of one its main revenue streams, the charge it used to make to consumers. As for the charge acting as a badge of trustworthiness, with online transactions unmediated by a salesman and customers able to service themselves, the need for customers to trust the company's recommendations is no longer there, because it is no longer making them.

The online service has a separate product offering, with forty-seven lenders offering mortgages on it at the time of writing, a figure which is constantly on the increase, and which includes pretty much all of the twenty-five biggest. It has its own product teams, its own sales people, and its own call centre. Having said that, the web does have a knock-on effect, generating leads for the physical business. The company is keenly aware that the removal of the charge to consumers online, and the consequent cutting out of the company's sales people, could alienate existing staff, so it wants to keep the two as integrated as possible. John Charcol estimates that for every mortgage arranged completely online, between one and one and a half others are researched online and then arranged through the company offline. That's still a pretty impressive number of people who are prepared to go through the whole process on the web, and calls into doubt the received wisdom that people do not trust the internet for high-value transactions.

It is also an example of the two sides of the business working together in harmony – collaboration is something which both parts of Charcol are keen to encourage. 'Quite often the two product development teams work together,' says Strauss. 'Often lenders give us special offers that they wouldn't give to the main business, because the main business does too much volume for them to experiment.' All very well for now, but soon it may not be, with the online side of the business expanding at such a speed.

With that expansion comes a change in the company's profile. The sort of people who are prepared to pay several hundred pounds for a traditional mortgage broker are different from those who'll pop online to check out the options for free. John Charcol has traditionally dealt mainly in high-end mortgages; below a certain level, it just wasn't worth the company's effort. Online, with no fee, the service is open to everyone, it's cheaper for John Charcol to administer, and the company can now make money from a far broader range of people.

It's an interesting example of how the role of intermediaries is changing. The internet is traditionally held to be bad for intermediaries: disintermediation, or cutting out the middle man, is a very popular bit of web jargon. In reality, a very large percentage of the companies that use the web in an intelligent and successful way are intermediaries of some sort. John Charcol is a classic example of this. The company realized that it made money because of a certain value it added, and set about thinking how it could exploit this online. It accepts that there will be cannibalization of its existing business, but sees that as an acceptable price to pay for the huge new vistas of opportunity that the internet opens up for it.

SOME GOOD NEWS

Intermediaries that are not perceived to add value by their customers, but are used solely through lack of choice (and here estate agents spring irresistibly to mind) are in trouble. Those that add value need to work out how that extra value can be transferred to this new medium. In addition, new intermediaries will come along to introduce efficiencies into fragmented markets, and shake up sectors where incumbents are complacent and don't add any value. John Charcol is an incumbent, but it sees itself as one of the agents of this kind of wind of change.

In many ways, John Charcol was already an internet company, years before it used the web. The type of service it offers – allowing users to compare products or services from a variety of different suppliers – is exactly the sort of thing the internet is good at. Have a look at Screentrade (www.screentrade.co.uk), which allows its users to fill in one form and get insurance quotes from several different financial services providers; or look at a comparison shopping service like ShopSmart (www.shopsmart.com), which allows people to compare prices for consumer products from a range of retailers. The sort of service John Charcol has always offered offline is not a million miles from this kind of thing. It was an internet business waiting to happen. Its natural tendency was always to be free for its customers to use, because that would open it up to a greater number of people. But before the internet came along, the economics weren't there which would allow the company to offer it for free; it had to support an expensive physical operation, with all the people and infrastructure costs incurred.

Strauss is already thinking about more ambitious ways in which the internet could shake up the way in which mortgages and other financial products are arranged. It's not just the customer interaction that can change, after all. The whole way in which the company brokers deals for customers could be different. He's already thinking about how John Charcol could move into brokering products like home and motor insurance. If it were to do so online, he reasons, with all the administrative efficiencies that would bring, it wouldn't have to just broker the deal and then leave it at that. It could rebroker it as regularly as it liked, every day if it wanted to. Suddenly, the company moves from being a one-off facilitator of a long-term financial product to a continuous, ongoing facilitator. And that would mean that it, rather than the lenders or insurers it deals with, would become the company that the consumer has the relationship with.

This kind of reworking of its business is still well into the future, but it shows how visionary the company is prepared to be in ensuring that it uses the internet to create value, rather than being wedded to a particular way of doing things. It's a mindset which has informed the company's successful transition into an online business so far.

Perhaps more than any other organization in the world, Procter & Gamble is the one that you'd expect to have the most problems adapting to the ramifications of the internet. The company is the world's biggest manufacturer of so-called fast-moving consumer goods: the sort of packaged products people buy in a supermarket. Its brands include everything from Ariel to Pantene, from Pringles to Pampers. The company, which was originally launched in 1837 as a Cincinnati soap and candle maker, now employs 110,000 people. Its products are sold in more than 140 countries, and it has operations in seventy of them.

Unsurprisingly, marketing lies at the heart of its business. The products it makes are relatively undifferentiated: the way it makes consumers want them is through advertising. The company was among the first ever to advertise on television, with an ad for its Ivory soap in the US, and it is still the world's biggest advertiser. Along with its arch rival Unilever, P&G was responsible for the existence of the soap opera, originally created to deliver a demographic that it could sell its products to. That's how hard-wired into the culture of traditional advertising the company is. Virtually everything it does is about the effectiveness of 30-second TV ads in selling its products.

Procter & Gamble has a vast, disparate product range, items that can't be transmitted digitally. It is almost impossible to sell them online – who's going to buy an individual box of washing powder over the internet, and more importantly, who's going to buy it from P&G, a company they're not used to having any meaningful relationship with? Their relationship is with the brands, not the company, and their transactional relationship is likely to be with a supermarket.

Added to this is a view of media that sees it as a place to advertise – to push brand messages one way, in the direction of the consumer. The company has no heritage of creating anything that people actually want to see – all its expertise is in shoving brand messages down the throats of a vast number of people in between entertainment content, largely against their will. Further, it knows that the messages will be irrelevant to most of them.

So when it comes to the internet, when it can't do that so easily, it hits a brick wall. Its ways of promoting its brands play to none of the strengths of the medium. The internet forces companies to give people things they want. They will only visit a web site if there's something in it for them, if they're likely to be interested when they get there. The customer is in charge. That forces companies to take account of them as individuals, tailoring the messages they send out so that they are appropriate to particular customers or customer groups. The ads traditionally created for a company like P&G are not compelling in their own right, and huge wastage is par for the course.

Then there's the organizational structure of a company like P&G, which is very rigid and hierarchical. It actively militates against the flux and flow of the internet. It makes it difficult to move fast, to recruit and retain the right kind of people. Such a company is almost certain to suffer from an ingrained organizational conservatism. If you've flourished and been a market leader for such a long time by doing things a certain way, where's the impetus to change? But change P&G has, and change in quite a profound way.

One man at the heart of this change was Frederic Colas. Until early 2000, when he left the company, he was in charge of P&G's European interactive operations. He was at the centre of what the company did with interactive media for over four years, joining it in 1996 as its first employee in the world with responsibility for interactive marketing, and set up P&G's entire European interactive operations in 1998. His personal history and that of P&G's internet operations are intimately intertwined.

Colas was never your typical P&G employee. He's loud, flamboyant and opinionated – very far from the identikit drones of P&G cliché. In fact, his willingness to talk with a journalist at all is pretty remarkable. One of the most noteworthy things about P&G as an organization is its insularity and lack of external communication. Put simply, it does not talk to the press. This change in itself is a symptom of the direction the company is moving in and the changes it is going through. When he spoke to me, shortly before leaving the company, Colas described those changes as being something that has shaken P&G to its very core. When he started out at the company, its attitude towards the internet bordered on outright hostility. On his first day – and arriving as a senior executive – he was given the key to his office, and the 'storeroom' label hadn't been removed from it. 'To even get internet access,' he told me, 'I needed the approval of the IT department and of a vice-president of the company. It took me three months to get internet access – and I was the internet guy.

'I was evangelizing within the company, and saying that everybody needs to get internet access. I had people saying back to me that one internet access terminal per department should be enough. Would they think that it was acceptable to have one phone per department?'

The first milestone on the way to enlightenment came at the beginning of 1997. 'I wrote a recom-

21

SOME GOOD
NEWS

mendation about the brand destination web site model as an advertising tool. The way it was thought of then was that you come to a web site, you see a history of Pringles, and you run out and buy a can of Pringles. The recommendation I wrote said that this model didn't make any sense at all. No one is interested in a can of Pringles. That's not what the brand is about at all.'

In other words, the company had fallen into the trap of viewing the internet as a broadcast, advertising medium. It had assumed that it would be able to use it in exactly the same way as it used television, to push brand messages at people and influence them to buy.

Its advertising-driven view of the medium was manifested elsewhere. At around this time, Procter & Gamble famously came out with a heretical view of online advertising. Unlike traditional advertising, where the advertiser pays for access to the entire audience of a TV programme, newspaper, or whatever, internet advertisers generally buy a subset of a particular site's audience. Typically, they pay a certain sum for every thousand times their ad is displayed to a user of that site. P&G's novel stance was that it would only pay for ads on the basis of the number of people who actually clicked on the ads and went through to a P&G-owned web site. The upshot of this was that it found it very difficult to get media-owning companies to accept its ads. The company was running the risk of ending up with a load of brand web sites that no one wanted to visit. This new medium didn't fit into traditional media ways of thinking. It was difficult to see what it could actually do for a company like P&G.

'My boss started to go through the whole clickthrough versus impressions debate,' comments

Colas. 'I was saying all along that this is a broader marketing issue, not just a media issue. Advertising on the internet was still part of the strategy, using a traditional advertising model. But at least it was going to where the audience was, rather than trying to create content which would attract an audience in its own right.'

Colas was still struggling to get his message across. The company formally set up an interactive department in April 1997. That may sound like a big step forward, but when Colas tried to push forward understanding of interactive media within the company, he found that his hands were still very definitely tied.

'I would go to, say, the agency that did the advertising for Pampers, which included the online advertising, and ask them what they'd learnt from a particular campaign. And they'd say that they could only tell me what they'd learnt if the Pampers brand manager allowed them to.

'As much as anything, it was a period of looking for money. In order to do anything with a particular brand, I had to try and get budget from the various divisions of the company. I was asking for money from individual brands. I remember one general manager of a division saying to me: "If I give you this money, I'll be fired." Eventually, I got some money to spend. I did things like getting one particular campaign half-funded by Intel, who were interested in pushing a particular technology forward, and so were willing to put half the money up.'

P&G Interactive was given its first big budget in September 1997, and for the first time, Colas was able to start to put a team in place. As well as continuing to test the effectiveness of online advertising, the department was able to start looking at how the internet affected wider business issues for the company.

'We defined that, in order to do successful advertising online, certain things have to be in place. Where you have to be convincing on TV and on other mass media, on the internet it's more important to be enticing than convincing. You have to mean something to people, rather than just make them believe that what you say is true. And you have to reward the consumer. That doesn't necessarily mean giving them product samples, coupons or whatever – it could mean giving them information, or something fun. It's about making sure that consumers don't feel that they've wasted their time.

'The dogma of internet marketing is: you're here to provide value to the consumer, because the consumer is in control. It's very different from traditional TV advertising, whose purpose is to convince you to buy the brand. It's not trying to give you value itself, or to change your life – because the product gives you the value, the product changes your life. On the internet, your messages must change people's lives, as well as persuading them to buy the product.'

This was a huge leap forward in the company's thinking. It was around this time that P&G started to think about how it should be tackling the internet in Europe. Armed with his experience of setting up an interactive department in the US, Colas returned to Europe and set up P&G Interactive Europe, based out of Brussels, in the summer of 1998. His mission was to push his mantra of creating engaging consumer experiences further and further forward. The emphasis was on using the medium to build a relationship with the consumer, to identify and target key consumer groups, to give them something of value, to tie them into an experience of, and a relationship with, the brand of a sort they could never have had through media like broadcast TV.

'All P&G's relationship marketing initiatives were led from Europe,' says Colas. 'I believe that relationship marketing is what this medium is made for. It's not about trying to reach everyone. It's about trying to reach certain specific but very important groups. It's about targeting, and it's about using data you've collected about those people to develop those relationships further. If you want to create a relationship with consumers, you have to be truly consumer-centric.

'Only a few of the company's brands could support a relationship marketing programme. They're the high-involvement brands – the brands for people, rather than the brands for things. So Pantene or Pampers could support it, but Ariel or Pringles couldn't.'

Some of the company's projects are taking the idea of relationship marketing to its logical conclusion. The best known is reflect.com, a web site based out of the US that offers its users personalized beauty advice. Personalization is at the heart of what the site is about. Reasoning that no one would visit a site about a particular beauty product, or buy specific beauty products individually from their manufacturer, the site instead offers a service. It's a destination in its own right, but one which people might actually want to go to, because it gives them beauty advice with a credibility that a site explicitly about a P&G brand never could. A site devoted to selling, say, Pantene

THE NET EFFECT

products would have too narrow a product range to appeal to consumers, and any beauty advice it gave would be perceived as untrustworthy. Rather than riding the coat tails of a particular brand, reflect.com is a brand in its own right. It's even structured as a separate company from Procter & Gamble. For the first time ever, P&G has spun off a project, which it only part owns. It did so partly because it needed to set the service up fast, and a spin-off could move faster than a P&G-owned venture, and also because it's an entirely new type of brand – one based on the experience of a service – that didn't fit into the existing P&G structure.

The move from products to services is something the big packaged-goods manufacturers have been thinking about for a while. You can't sell a tube of toothpaste or a box of nappies individually over the internet. But you could sell a bathroom replenishment service, or a complete babycare service. And then you can build other services around those things, services that take you into areas you've never occupied before. If you sell babycare services, a babysitting ring could be tacked onto it. Suddenly you have a much more intimate relationship with your customers. P&G's great rival Unilever has been trialling a service called myhome.com, a complete home-cleaning offering, using Unilever products Jif and Persil. It's a dramatic move. In order to develop and extend its relationship with the consumer, Unilever is prepared to go as far as getting itself a fleet of vans and employing people to go into its customers' homes. Unilever has acknowledged that in the future, in order to sell a product, it may be necessary to wrap it up in a service.

Companies like P&G and Unilever have realized

that they have to be about a lot more than a box of soap powder on someone's shelf. To be a brand on the internet, they have to be about an experience.

P&G's other venture in this area, swizzle.co.uk, is a joint venture with internet search engine, portal provider and media company Excite, to target the teenage girl market in the UK. Like reflect.com, it's a recognition by the company that on the internet, consumers have a wealth of information at their fingertips. They're empowered to make decisions in ways they never have been before. They're much less likely to just sit there and passively soak up whatever companies throw at them. So companies whose business is built around creating products and then promoting them heavily with one-way advertising are forced to change. It cuts to the heart of their business, something which Colas claims P&G now recognizes.

Speaking during his last weeks with P&G, he said, 'We're now creating a digital business. It's gone from being about media, to being about marketing, to being about business. Now our thinking is that it changes our business model. Everybody in P&G is convinced, right up to the very top, that this is going to profoundly change the way we do business. It makes us do entirely new things like reflect.com, things that we'd never have even thought about doing before the internet. But it affects the business on other levels as well. It accelerates things like brand development. It makes us think about how we interface with our suppliers and customers. It makes us think about how we work inside the company. We have had to become open instead of hierarchical. We have had to start doing things, getting them to market quickly, instead of just testing them.

'The business units are starting to invest a lot themselves. They have to just do it, because they need to succeed in it. They will invent what success is in this market. We're entering a new era, where this is becoming mainstream.'

P&G is moving towards experience-based brands. In exactly the same way as the company used advertising to give its products unique brand qualities, so Colas believes that the uniqueness of its internet activities will be its greatest advantage in the digital era.

'P&G's big advantage is that, at the end of the day, we're doing things that only a few people can do. We're not going to go bankrupt. I'd be much more scared if I was M&S or someone, because retailing is so easy – anyone can do it, so you're much more open to new competitors.'

If this sounds like the airily dismissive talk of someone on one side of the classic producer-retailer fence, perhaps it is. But look at the internet-only companies that have been most successful: an awful lot of them are, primarily, retailers. Retailers are by their nature intermediaries, brokers, a layer between the production of goods and services and their consumption. As brokers, they are in a position to be challenged, and a number of online players are trying to do just that. Auction sites like QXL and eBay, for example, provide a market-place where people can trade; it's an alternative intermediary. Collaborative buying sites like letsbuyit.com, which encourage people to buy in big groups and then negotiate bulk discounts with suppliers, are in effect doing exactly the same thing that retailers do. Buying wholesale in bulk and then selling retail individually is precisely their game. Collaborative buying services are trying to do the same, but to be driven directly by consumer demand, asking people what they want rather than trying to guess what they might want.

All this doesn't mean that retailers will be cut out completely and go out of business. It just means that they have to add value. Colas's point is that a company like P&G adds value by creating something which can be sold; there is value in its branded products and services. It has a physical dimension which cannot be replaced. The same is not true for every sort of company.

If retailers really are under threat from the internet, then Marks & Spencer is in a lot of trouble. Every article these days refers to it as 'the troubled retailer'. Profits have dipped, true, but more importantly, its hold on the British psyche as a byword for quality and reliability also seems to be slipping. Its slowness to embrace the internet could be seen as a classic symptom of the company's risk-averse attitude to business. M&S has done what it has done very successfully for a long time, so why should it change? The answer is that if it doesn't embrace the internet as a key business channel, other companies will, and it will lose market share.

For a company supposedly suffering from fundamental problems, M&S's current financial situation isn't exactly horrendous. It turned in a profit of £500m in 1999; let's face it, most internet companies would kill for a profit of £5. M&S may not be quite the force it was, but it's still vast, still serving more than three-quarters of the entire UK population in any given month.

In truth, the internet wouldn't have to account for a large percentage of M&S's business to make it one of the biggest forces in British e-tailing. Direct selling in general makes up a very small percentage of the company's business. Marks & Spencer's total UK turnover last year (1999) was £6.2 billion. If only 10 per cent of that were direct sales, the company would be the biggest catalogue business in the UK. It wouldn't take much more than one per cent to make it the country's biggest internet seller.

If the downward movement of M&S's profits really is a sign of impending doom, and if the company is going to be eaten by online players, then it's not going to happen for a few years yet. And in the meantime, the company has plenty of leeway to turn itself around. It's something M&S is trying to do right now, and the net is one of the ways it's doing so.

Peter Robinson, the company's head of e-commerce, is a surprisingly talkative man. Like Procter & Gamble, Marks & Spencer's reluctance to talk about what it's doing is legendary. It rarely talks to the press, and until recently it didn't advertise. The implication is that everyone knows what the M&S brand is all about, what the company does and what it stands for, so why would it need to go out of its way to tell people about itself? Suddenly, though, when it comes to the internet, no one is quite so sure what M&S is all about any more. The company is a retailer, so there's an expectation that it must make some kind of positive move to sell online. For a number of years, however, the company was silent. To the outsider, it didn't seem to be doing anything in particular. In fact, M&S behind the scenes has been beavering away at an internet strategy for years. That the company has suddenly felt the need to start talking about what it's doing is telling. For the first time in decades, people weren't sure what M&S's strategy was, and so external communication became important.

Robinson accepts that the company has been a relative latecomer to the internet party. It's something which has been a source of frustration to e-commerce operators. M&S has just about the most trusted brand in the UK. That makes it perfect for online retailing. More people would be prepared to make their first online purchase from M&S than from any other company. If the company really pushed e-commerce, there's a good chance that it would expand the market for selling over the internet as a whole in the UK.

The company's perceived slowness doesn't worry Robinson, though. He doesn't feel that M&S has lost out on much. Far more important to a company like M&S than speed to market, he insists, is ensuring that its web presence is made to fit with the rest of its business – and that meant it had to move slowly.

'The biggest decision that we made was that we decided to see integration across all channels as the future,' he says. 'We felt that the customer wanted a relationship with us across all the channels that are available to them. It wasn't about there not being any shops any more. It was about striking the right balance. We felt that our customers had a relationship with the M&S brand, and that they would want the different channels to be working together. That was our view right from the start.

'Yes, there's a real advantage in being able to move more quickly by spinning off your internet operations. You can concentrate on going much, much faster. You don't have to integrate everything you do into business systems, into processes, into rules. So we did have a long debate at the start about the different ways we could do it. We eventually took the view that while it might allow us to move more quickly, it wouldn't allow us to meet customers' expectations. If you have a business like ours, and you want to meet those expectations, you simply can't move that quickly. And when you have a brand as strong as ours, meeting those expectations is the most important thing you have to do.

'We have to give people options. The customer will look for the easiest route to get the information and the service they want. The easiest route for them and the easiest for us are not always the same.'

The result is that the internet operation is completely integrated with the company's stores. Prices are the same, and delivery is handled by individual stores. In effect, the customer still has the relationship with their local store; the web site is an extension of each of these stores, not a separate retailing operation in its own right. This, combined with the softly-softly approach the company has taken to developing its internet presence, could be seen as a fudge, a hedge strategy designed just to sidestep channel conflict until it inevitably comes back to haunt the company later.

However, with a brand as strong as M&S, it would be overstating it to say that its delay has harmed it that badly. Add in the dotcom shakeout of early 2000, when confidence in the prospects of internet-only players ebbed and the future suddenly didn't seem quite so inevitably digital, and M&S's decision to take its time and spend a while working out the most appropriate way for it to tackle the internet, rather than rush headlong into launching a poorly-branded and poorly-integrated site, began to look more sensible.

'In amongst all the hype, we had enough information from experiments we had done to know that volumes were actually still very low,' says Robinson. 'The figures don't match up to anything like what people would expect. We knew that we wouldn't lose out on that much if we took a bit of time to make sure we got it right.

'One of the reasons we have taken it at a sensible pace is that there's a risk of fringe activity damaging your core activity. We've tried to strike a balance between moving quickly enough, and not becoming too anxious and being seduced into damaging our brand by moving too quickly.'

If you're a dotcom, you haven't got much to lose if you just weigh in and do as much as you can, as soon as you can, because you have no existing business to damage. If you're a company with an established reputation – and here M&S is about as extreme an example as you can get – protecting that brand is the most important thing you have to do. That means making sure that you're 100 per cent certain that anything you're going to do online is perfect before you do it. If a consumer's experience of M&S online is bad, that damages their perception of the brand as a whole. And as Robinson points out, with the sort of volumes we've been talking about in the short life-span of the internet so far, that's not worth the risk. Yes, M&S has been slow. But it's been slow precisely because it has so much to lose. It simply cannot afford to get anything wrong – as good a reason for caution as any.

SOME GOOD NEWS

The other reason for caution is, inevitably, its desire to avoid channel conflict. M&S takes the view that there simply cannot be any disjunction between what it does online and what it does offline. The whole way the company has approached the internet is based around a fundamental desire to avoid channel conflict, because it values its stores so highly. It's one of the problems old-economy operators are saddled with, but in the case of a company like M&S it is also its great strength. It would be an odd inversion of business logic which saw a hugely successful store-based retailing operation as an encumbrance. It's actually the biggest trump card M&S has online, and the company's desire to build on that strength is only to be expected. The trick for the company will be to make sure it doesn't cling obstinately to existing channels in a way which makes it impossible to embrace new ones. So as well as trying as far as possible to integrate its internet department into the main business, it is also trying to integrate its online selling into its main retail channel.

Robinson is very clear of the advantages the M&S stores give the company: 'There are many things that customers will still want to do in stores. We have a very high refund rate – people don't want to wait in for ages for someone to come round and collect items they don't want, or whatever. People like to walk into a shop, take something back and get instant credit. That kind of thing will be a big problem for pure e-commerce companies.

'With a lot of products – take something like a bed – the point of purchase and the point of order are often very different. You might order something from one place and get it delivered from another. Or you might do your research in one place and buy somewhere else. So you have to keep the channels integrated. People can go and order online after trying it out in the shop. We have to separate out the influence-to-buy element of the transaction from the actual purchase. It could equally work the other way round. We only have beds in twenty-five of our stores, and the range you can research online is big, so people might do their initial search online and then come into the shop to buy.'

The key for M&S, according to Robinson, is correctly identifying what it wants its online presence to do. All established retailers face a decision. They have to work out which customer group they're after. If a company just transfers its existing customers to the internet, that can be fine, as long as each transaction is cheaper to administer there, the saving from doing without stores outweighing the costs of setting up and running a web site and delivering to people's homes. But a lot of companies want to use the internet to widen their audience.

The big retailers are all in this game. Tesco is on record as saying that it wants to use its web site to attract the sort of people who can't stand supermarket shopping. The company's online store is not there to service anyone who willingly stalks its aisles in search of bargains once a week or more. It's after a different group of shoppers, who don't have the time or inclination to walk, drive or catch a bus to a store, traipse around loading up a trolley, queue at the till and make their way home again only to find that they've forgotten half the items they meant to buy. (You may spot the bitter voice of experience here.) The company wants its web presence to be the best

36
THE NET EFFECT

place for those people to shop online. It's a laudable aim. The sort of people without the time for supermarket shopping stand a better than average chance of having a large income, and in fact the average per-customer spend in Tesco's online store has traditionally been around twice as high as in one of its physical stores.

Another of the big high-street grocery retailers, Iceland, has used the internet even more starkly in its attempts to address different customer groups. The company has long been saddled with a reputation for selling only cheap frozen goods (in fact, the company still officially trades under the name 'Iceland Frozen Foods'). That skews the profile of its customers towards poorer, lower-spending groups, and means that while its stores serve a high number of customers, the average spend of each one is extremely low by supermarket standards at around £10 per visit. It has been trying to change this with a big branding push. This isn't a cosmetic move. Fresh food now makes up more than 50 per cent of the products in its stores. In addition, Iceland was the first big UK multiple to ban genetically modified ingredients from its own-label products, and now sells only organic vegetables.

Another plank of the rebranding has been a big push for the internet market. The company operates one of the biggest home shopping grocery services in the UK, which is unusual in offering free delivery. It has integrated the iceland.co.uk web address into the name on its storefronts. Iceland wants to broaden its customer base, and sees the internet as an ideal place to do so. Like Tesco, the results so far have been impressive. Where the average customer to one of its physical stores spends £10, its average customer online spends a massive £60. This is partly because the company specifies a minimum spend of £40 for people buying online as the quid pro quo for free delivery. The minimum order value could mean that it is attracting higher-spending customers, in the more affluent socio-economic groups that the company wants to target. Or it could just mean that customers are piling up goods in their online shopping baskets, and just waiting until they cross the minimum order threshold before buying. That would make each order cheaper to process, but it would also reduce the number of times the company has contact with its customers. And having regular contact with customers is the lifeblood of supermarkets. It's the time when they get to use their expertise in merchandising, cross-selling, and all the ways in which they can squeeze more money out of people than they were intending to spend – all the things which make them skilled retailers, rather than just companies with big warehouses full of products.

For a company like M&S, increasing the number of people it serves isn't easy. It already serves 76 per cent of the UK population every month. Convincing the rest to come and shop with the company is going to require a lot of effort, probably for a relatively small return. For that reason, M&S has decided to make its existing customers the focus of its internet service – hence the decision to keep the internet integrated with the channel those people already use, the stores. Says Robinson: 'The way we view it is that there's an opportunity for us to sell more to our best customers by offering them a better service. We can create more best customers. We can get those people to increase their spend. We can work out what's making them good customers, and work on that. If you're looking at customer segmentation, then what we want to do is move more people into the "best customers" segment.'

While that may be the company's aim in the UK, overseas it expects its focus to be on expansion. Where the UK internet operation is about providing more channels for loyal customers, there's a genuine opportunity to build a new customer base abroad. The company currently generates a couple of billion pounds of annual sales across thirty countries. Its core customers overseas tend to be expatriates and anglophiles, and Robinson sees the chance to reach a greater number of these people online, in places where the company doesn't have physical stores, as a tremendous opportunity. 'We can get to these people if we link up with the right passion areas,' he says. But he insists that the company has to get the infrastructure in place to sell in those countries before it presses on with an international e-commerce push. 'Our capability in those countries needs to come first. The customers come after that. There's a big opportunity for us to direct-sell internationally, and we see that being electronic rather than paper based.'

The internet opens up the world for M&S. It gives it the chance to reach more customers, and to turn existing customers into better customers. Relationships should be at the heart of everything a company does on the internet.

M&S may have looked like it was moving too slowly. But it is waking up from its slumbers, it's still in a position to take hold of the market and lead it. Robinson is certainly confident. 'Last year [1999] was all about the dotcoms. This year is all about the sleeping giants waking up. We've still got a lot of learning to do, but we'll get there, and then we'll take the lead.'

The internet is incredibly young. In terms of its effects on the business world, we're a tiny way down a very, very long road. But for some companies, it's already been a rollercoaster ride. Encyclopaedia Britannica is a case in point. The company has undergone two massive changes in response to digital media and changed everything about itself in an attempt to re-invent what it does for the future. It's been incredibly visionary, and yet it still has problems. I'm going to talk at some length about Britannica, because it's a fascinating tale.

The company first came to my attention two years ago. Actually, that's a lie – along with a very sizeable percentage of the earth's inhabitants, I've been aware of Encyclopaedia Britannica and its awesome compendium of knowledge ever since I can remember. But it became a company I followed with interest in 1998, when it took the rather dramatic step of laying off its entire door-to-door direct sales force. This is a move akin to McDonald's firing Ronald, for the salesmen were the people synonymous with the brand. They had entered into folklore, with their indescribable pushiness and refusal to accept 'no' for an answer. They even had a Monty Python sketch written about them, the one where a Britannica salesman pretends to be a Jehovah's Witness in order to gain access to a potential customer's home. For Britannica to get rid of the whole lot signalled a wholesale change in the way the business thought about itself and about its future.

Something had happened to the company, and that something was digital media. In terms of a business having to turn itself round to accommodate the changes foisted on it by the digital era, it's about as extreme an example as you could wish for. And does it have a happy ending? Well, read on and then decide.

Britannica has been around for more than 230 years. It has changed ownership numerous times, but its core business has always been printed encyclopaedias, and for a long time, its door-to-door sales force was at the heart of selling them. There were two reasons why Britannica decided to shed what had been such an important part of its business: the internet and CD-Roms. CDs happened first. The company had been the world's biggest supplier of encyclopaedia products for as long as anyone could remember. Then, halfway through the 1990s, it suddenly wasn't any more. And what was particularly galling for the company was the identity of the interloper that had knocked it off the top of the tree: Microsoft. The world's biggest software company may sound like an unlikely repository of knowledge, but its Encarta product was more widely distributed than Britannica, and although it may not have had quite the same heritage or wielded quite the same authority, that was still a shock to the company's system. The reason Encarta was able to be top dog had nothing at all to do with its content. It was entirely to do with the way it was distributed. Encarta was a CD-based product, and it was given away with millions of computers that had Microsoft's Windows operating system installed on them. Microsoft, of course, insists that it is not given away, and that the price of Encarta is factored into the overall price of the PCs it is bundled with; in any event Britannica found that it was no longer the world's biggest supplier of encyclopaedia information. The value of its business had rested on the scarcity of that information, and the difficulty and expense of getting hold of the books that contained it. That scarcity was fast disappearing.

Jason Plent, managing director of Britannica.co.uk, is a man with belief in his business. He becomes animated when he talks about the direction the company is moving in, and the exciting products it will be able to offer in the future. And he cheerfully admits that the journey the company has been through over the last few years has been rough, rocky and disorientating. 'We've changed more in the last three to four years than we did in the previous 230,' he admits. Addressing the effect the popularity of CDs had on the company, he says: '$650m had dropped off our value quite quickly as people switched to buying CDs. So we had to change what we did.'

The answer was to focus Britannica's efforts on CDs. That meant moving from a thick set of printed books costing between £1,000 and £3,000 to a disk of metal costing £49. The company had to do it, because Encarta was in a powerful position, despite its lack of history. Plent is predictably dismissive of Encarta's content, but it was clearly taken seriously by Britannica – you don't turn your entire business model on its head to counter something that you don't see as a threat.

'What was clever with Encarta was the distribution,' he comments. 'We've been head-to-head with them for years. In order to keep pace with us, and to keep up that distribution, they had to localize their content – the problem they had with their content as it stood was that it was low-quality and too general. Unfortunately, they localized to a rather alarming degree. In the Italian version, they have an Italian, Antonio Meucci, as the inventor of the telephone – they said that he only failed to get credited with the invention because he forgot to send the patent off. But in the UK and US versions, it's Bell who invented it.

'Our editorial policy is to state truths where there's no dispute, or to give options where there is.'

Having accommodated that cataclysmic change into its business, Britannica was soon forced to accommodate another. The reason was – you guessed it – the web, because the web is good at exactly the same thing Britannica is good at, information. And, as with CDs, the ubiquity and easy availability of that information was a problem for the company – with the web, even more so.

Knowledge used to be the preserve of a few, and acquiring it was a difficult and time-consuming task. Britannica was one of the gatekeepers of knowledge. Acquiring a set of the encyclopaedia was an autodidact's dream. It was one of the few ways of finding out about almost anything.

Now, there isn't much you can't find out given half an hour with a PC and a web browser. Information is no longer precious in and of itself. The value is in how trustworthy its source is, and how easy it is to navigate and find.

In the context of a medium full of freely available information on every subject being adopted by a mass of people, it became clear to Britannica that it would struggle in the future to base a business entirely on charging for access to information, whether that be in books or on a CD. That took the company inexorably in the direction of the conclusion that it should do about the most radical thing it could, and run contrary to 230 years of history by giving its content away for free.

So, from three grand to fifty quid to nothing. Quite a path to tread in less than half a decade. In October 1999, the company was divided into two. Britannica Inc, based in Chicago, would be responsible for the production of encyclopaedia content. Britannica.com would be a provider of intelligent information services on the internet. The company, and its subsidiaries such as Britannica.co.uk, would license content from Britannica Inc. And how would it make its money? Well, that's where it became interesting.

The company identified several revenue streams. It would make money from the syndication of key intellectual property that the company possesses, such as demographic information which could be sold on to other companies. Fine – not earth-shattering, but fine. It would also look at retaining some sort of subscription element, possibly for the company's educational service, where schools who are happy to pay a subscription fee can do so if they would prefer the content they're given to be free from commercial interests, and fenced off from some of the, shall we say, less educationally relevant material on the web. Once again perfectly reasonable, but unlikely to be enough to support a flourishing business. Then there are traditional book sales, albeit at a very low level, and CD sales. Both of those will eventually fall as the free online service becomes more popular, but the CDs could still have a place within schools or libraries, for the reasons outlined above, as well as being sold to

43

SOME GOOD
NEWS

people without web access. In fact, in the short period since the online service has been available for free in the US, CD sales have picked up considerably, with schools and parents the main buyers.

The key revenue stream for Britannica, however, would be advertising. The company would accept ads on the site. The corollary of advertising revenues would be sponsorship, and e-commerce, offering products for sale via deals with third parties to give those companies access to Britannica's audience. According to Plent, it is advertising which replaces paid-for content as the company's main revenue stream, at least in the short term. He also claims that the Britannica.com site is regularly sold out of inventory for up to six months ahead, regularly turns down advertisers it doesn't think fit with its brand, and can afford to refuse to offer discounts on its ad rates.

So, the company has gone from being a print publisher that charges people for bits of paper with words on them, bound together into books, to a media organization that makes its money by providing an audience to advertisers. Turn-arounds don't get much more radical than that. It means that, instead of competing with its traditional book publisher rivals, or even with the likes of Encarta, Britannica was competing with anyone that gives content away online and tries to support it with advertising. Specifically, the nature of the product it now offers – a complete information solution which also helps users to find useful information and services on other web sites – positions it very close to some of the biggest internet-spawned brands: what used to be called search engines and online services, but now seem to prefer the name portals. And the market dominated by likes of Yahoo,

Excite, AltaVista, MSN and AOL is a pretty difficult one to muscle in on.

The first time I met the urbane and affable Plent, in March 1999, he came across as a characteristically confident new-economy boss figure. Few people in the internet space lack self-belief, or belief in the ability of their companies to inherit the earth. A lot of internet players have just lived through a crazy, surging spurt of economic growth, with themselves at the centre. It's no surprise that they are confident in their own abilities.

And so much of the internet economy is based on confidence. With most of the new players far from turning in a profit, appearances are all. The demeanour and perceived competence of a company's bosses are absolutely crucial. If you don't think you're going to be the most successful company of all time, especially in the middle of *this*, why should anyone else have any confidence in you? You have to be seen to be the biggest, the strongest, the most aggressive, the most confident.

Britannica may not be a company spawned out of the dotcom explosion, but Plent certainly had the necessary new-economy bullishness about the future for britannica.co.uk, the UK subsidiary of britannica.com. He had been in the job for only a few months when we met and talked in the company's Soho offices, but he was clearly thrilled by the pace of change and enthused by the direction the company was taking. Even the troubled launch of the US site, which crashed rather spectacularly after the company had failed to properly test its resilience, was a cause for celebration.

'Obviously, the biggest thing this company has ever experienced was when our service went free,' he says.

'We launched our US consumer service in October 1999, and it was a tremendous success straight away. We had an incredible amount of traffic. It was so many more people than we expected, and of course, we experienced some problems with not being able to cope with that demand.

'It was incredible to see the power that the brand has. We got so much traffic partly because we generated so much PR coverage. We were in the broadsheet press all over the world, in Britain and America, but also in the rest of Europe and even Latin America.'

At the time Plent and I met, the company's US site was receiving between twenty and thirty million page impressions (the number of times any page on the site is accessed) a month. That's not quite in the top tier of internet media sites like Yahoo and Excite, but it's respectable enough and it's certainly enough to make plenty of money from advertising, particularly if, as Plent claims, all the available inventory on the site was sold out.

Interestingly, only about half of the site's visitors were from the US, the other half being spread around the rest of the world. So the US site was already doing a pretty good job of serving a UK audience, even without britannica.co.uk. The site also had one of those rare and much talked-about internet qualities, stickiness. That means, essentially, how long people stay there. A lot of time and effort is expended trying to make sites sticky, and what makes them sticky is, broadly speaking, engaging content. Anything over five minutes is generally considered pretty impressive; visitors to britannica.com were spending an average of twenty minutes there.

Plent, unsurprisingly enough, got quite inspired when talking about what the new Britannica sites could do, and what they would be able to do.

'Britannica.com has been built on a global infrastructure, and that's been built over two years. It's based on key intellectual property assets. Yes, that will include the encyclopaedia, but what it's really going to be is a knowledge portal aimed at high-earning, high-intellect consumers. It's the world's largest encyclo-paedia, but it's also the world's largest thesaurus, with 250,000 terms in it. So when you access content about, say, Buddhism, you'll find lots of other relevant, cross-referenced content. That cross-referencing isn't done by some piece of technology – it's been hand-built by academics over 232 years.

'Now we can build out, and add in contemporary stuff, and create new content based around particular events. We have deals to take content from people like the *Washington Post*, *Newsweek*, the *New Statesman*, *The Economist* and Guardian Unlimited (the online version of the *Guardian* newspaper), and we're working on others, especially on ones outside the US. Then we also have databases of people, places, events, things.

'We can combine all of that. We can take the mystery out of searching. Search engines don't work, everyone knows that. It's difficult for people to find anything using them.'

He is equally dismissive of the big search sites' attempts to turn themselves into so-called 'portals', taking content from a variety of sources and aggregating it in one place, arguing that 'anyone can do that'.

'We will make a difference,' he insists. 'We'll be in the place between the crawling, algorithmic search engines, and those who provide niche information on particular subjects. It's free, it covers everything, and it does it better than everything else. It has all the things that other web portals have: e-mail, news, stock prices etc. But we also have things that nobody else has: we have our content, and we have it indexed.

'And more than anything, we have our brand. People know who we are, they want to work with us, and our brand associations are all about quality. The brand stands for ethereal values. If you talk to someone about the Britannica brand, you get a couple of minutes of them talking about book salesmen putting their foot in your door and all that. But then, when they think about it, they talk about Britannica as a repository of knowledge, and an authoritative one. People say: "I would trust anything from that company." Nobody can do all the things we can do. We're not just the biggest, we're the best.'

Inspiring stuff – very media-friendly, and good for rallying the troops. Plent really does make it all sound a very long way from that bits-of-paper and foot-in-door salesmen image of old. On one level, the company has completely changed what it does and everything that it is. But on another level, it hasn't changed that much at all. The format, the distribution mechanism are different. The way in which the company makes money is different. But what has stayed the same is the content and the brand. Britannica's brand has always been about providing a breadth and depth of content that people instinctively trust. In re-inventing itself as a provider of knowledge and information services on the internet, Britannica has recognized that it is in that brand – not in nicely-bound volumes of books that it can charge three grand for – that its value lies. As Plent says, the medium the company originally chose to distribute its content was really just an accident of history.

'Our business has been about aggregation all the way,' he says. 'If you think about it, we got the best academics to write the best articles and made them available on the best medium available at the time, which happened to be paper. Then the best medium became the CD, and then it became the internet. It's aggregation at speed. We're very good at getting information together and putting it out quickly on the best available medium. Now we have an umbrella organization, britannica.com, which is there specifically to do that.'

The company is not going to abandon other forms of distributing its content. The free-content model and the internet may be where it perceives its future to lie, but paid-for media like CDs and even books will continue to play a part in what it does. Just because it wants to position itself as a key player in the new economy, Britannica hasn't thrown out the baby with the bathwater and got rid of its old business completely. After all, the books still make money. They now account for just 5 per cent of the company's sales in the UK, but that varies from territory to territory, and there are some places where print will continue to be incredibly important for the company for a long time to come.

Plent comments: 'The owner of the company is adamant about books – we will not abandon them while there's still a market for them. Think about places like China, where there are very few computers. Books will carry on being big for us there.'

Britannica is changing to adapt to changing

THE NET EFFECT

conditions, but the change can still be characterized as reactive. If it had been able to carry on as before, it would happily have done so. It only made the decision to turn itself around because of the arrival of new and unexpected competitors: on CD, the likes of Encarta; and on the internet, potentially everybody in the world. The company was lucky in so far as the advent of the digital era, and with it the biggest ever challenge to the way the company does business, coincided with a change of ownership and a positive attitude to all things digital. Britannica was bought by an American private investor in 1996, and since then all the decisions about its direction have come from the very top.

'The guy who owns the company had the vision to see that it had a good brand and good core assets. That was at a time when we were still in the position to become the biggest provider of encyclopaedia CDs quickly, and also get online and start to dominate there quickly as well,' comments Plent.

He adds that motivating staff was a challenge, because they suddenly found themselves doing something they'd never done before, but that the sense of a vision for the company from the very top made that task easier. 'We really had to put a firework up people – to make them realize how important it was for us to be competitive. And to make them realize that we were going to be in a completely different business. It has been a complete revolution. Not a bloody or violent one, but a successful re-engineering of what we do.'

At every level, there have been changes in the way Britannica does things. As the focus of the business has shifted onto a different medium, and the way in which it expects to make its money has correspondingly changed, so the business has experienced a ripple-effect in the way it operates.

For instance, it now has a greater depth of content, because it doesn't labour under the same space constraints – if it is well-organized, more is always more when it comes to content on the web. The print version of the encyclopaedia had around forty-five million definitions in it. Online, that rose to between fifty-five and sixty-five million in a period of under three years. This is an unheard-of pace of change for the company; traditionally, it has worked on business cycles of around twelve years, a time span dictated by the regularity with which it could update its content. Suddenly, the company has had to work a lot faster, and with a lot more focus, than it has ever had to work before.

It has also changed the way in which it speaks to people around the world. In the past, the focus of the company was the English language; its roots are in Scotland and it has, down the years, been both a British and an American company. But it has always embodied a certain kind of occidental world-view – that was just accepted by its global readership. Now, on the internet, the company has to address a variety of different audiences around the world in a way more tailored to local cultures. Britannica Inc now publishes content in eleven languages, and expanding the foreign language content element of what it does is one of the company's big priorities as it grows. That means changing the way it thinks about content, says Plent. 'In the past, if we'd had an article about a subject like, say, Buddhism, it would have been written by a UK or US academic. They'd have been the best academic in those countries to write the article, but they'd still have been from those countries. On the internet, the new company has to be truly international, to talk to people all over the world, and so we had to make the way our content was written truly international to reflect that. So the piece on Buddhism would be written by a leading Buddhist in Tibet, say.'

The plan was ambitious in the extreme. The company was looking to launch britannica.co.uk officially in the third quarter of 2000. A launch in Australia was due sooner still, and the company had opened an office in India with a view to launching there as speedily as possible, too.

The speed of movement forced on the company by the new economy had tightened up its business practices across the board. It had gone from a twelve-year development cycle for core content to a three-year one, and that would impact even on its print products, with the next print version of the encyclopaedia expected some time in 2002 or 2003 – far quicker than it would ever have moved before.

After rolling its consumer service out globally and using that to reposition the organization, the company was intending to focus on the education market. Just to give a few examples of the powerful relationships it has in that market: Britannica has access, through tie-ups with educational institutions, to 52 per cent of people in the US education system, a potential 45m people. Similarly, the entire Danish school system has access to the company's content, as does the whole of the Norwegian university system, and all the schools, universities and libraries in Iceland. Plent spoke confidently about a richer experience for educational users, with the content from the main print title supplemented by a directory of 170,000 educational web sites, a thesaurus, a dictionary, and all sorts of additional projects like indexes of curricula, study guides and so on.

I was impressed. Here, it seemed, was a company that had isolated what it did well, what people valued it for, where its brand lay, and had worked out what those things meant in this new environment. The company seemed to have dotcommed itself from top to toe, and not in a gratuitous way. Using the internet as its main channel to supply information made perfect sense, and the change in business model was an inevitable consequence of that. Moreover, in Plent the British arm of the company seemed to have a driven leader with self-belief, who reflected the vision of the company's future which was filtering down from the very top. Everything seemed right. The company would launch britannica.co.uk and enter the field of British online media in an aggressive way. My only concern was whether the company could sustain a real, long-term business based on advertising revenue and the like. The UK's online media scene is massively overcrowded, with far more supply than demand. So many sites were being populated with content and funded by advertising; all too often it's the revenue stream that web companies cling to when they can't think of any other way to make money out of what they do.

None the less, there were one or two other possible sources of revenue for Britannica that had promise, and besides, what choice did the company have? It had to embrace the internet era. It wouldn't survive in any meaningful form, at any meaningful size, if it didn't. And the way it had embraced it seemed to me to be measured, considered and logical, not just a knee-jerk leap into dark uncharted digital waters because its old boat was sinking. I thought it had a raft.

A few weeks later, that raft started to spring a leak. It was a few weeks before britannica.co.uk was due to launch, and one of my colleagues at *Revolution* received an e-mail from a contact. 'Just heard that Britannica are going to pull the plug on their UK site before it's even launched,' it said. Plent regretfully conceded that it was true. The company had decided to ditch britannica.co.uk, along with the other planned sites in Australia and India, and use britannica.com as its worldwide site. So much of the traffic to britannica.com was already coming from Europe that the company had to come to the conclusion that a massive investment in localized content creation didn't add up. The company would look again at britannica.co.uk in late 2000, but it didn't sound hopeful. As for all the editorial and technological staff that supposedly embodied the heart and soul of the new company, the real value it provided to its customers – well, many of them were going to be out of a job. A third of its staff were laid off, most of them from the editorial department. The company would continue to rely on the academic content which had always been its bedrock in print, supplemented by content from its deals with third parties, but it would no longer have a big team creating UK content to go with it.

What are we to make of the Britannica story? There are a number of possible reactions. One is to see this as a shuddering reverse, evidence that the company hadn't thought out its proposition and was forced into a rethink and a withdrawal, the grandiose plans for localized content hastily abandoned. Equally, it could be seen as a positive thing: Britannica.com was strong enough to have global appeal, so why waste money on local operations?

The company has undergone a series of strategic rethinks, culminating with the decision to shelve britannica.co.uk. Is it an admission of defeat? A brave acknowledgement that the company's UK operation was over-resourced? A function of the inevitable globalization of companies' operations that the internet brings about? A visionary attempt to run a slimline business with a whole new set of revenue streams and a dramatically reduced cost base? A failure to see the future coming? Or is it all of these things? Is it an example of a company perfectly understanding the business it is in, the value that it brings, the things its customers want, and constantly adapting and evolving to take that into account, even when that means changing strategy, and then ditching that strategy shortly before launch? Or is it an example of a company getting caught quite spectacularly on the hop and repeatedly leaping like a scalded kitten until it found a place it could safely rest? Is this an old-world company admirably pulling its business round, or a slightly desperate and over-hasty attempt to ditch 230-odd years of heritage to do something completely different, which has ultimately moved too fast for an old-economy company like Britannica? Or is it a combination of good and bad, with the UK operation unable to pull its weight but the US continuing to do so? And wouldn't it be the most ironic twist of the information age if a company like that, with a heritage like that and a name like that, was not only owned by Americans but ran all its operations out of America and flourished there? The internet does not respect any sort of frontier, geographical ones included.

The answer to all these question is: no one knows – yet. This is the great joy and the great conundrum of the internet and its economy. No one knows what will happen. It is all up in the air. It's what makes life so difficult for companies trying to make sense of the new challenges the internet presents them with. Britannica is one of the starkest examples I can find of a company which has undergone several convoluted processes of change as it struggles to come to terms with it all. The new economy has moved with its characteristic speed, and Britannica, a giant of the old economy, has tried to pull itself round and adapt. In doing so, it has tried to turn itself into a new-economy company. It could emerge as a powerful new information provider, the definitive source of information on the most information-rich medium the world has ever seen. Or it could end up wishing that the internet had never happened to it, and it could have just carried on merrily publishing big fat expensive books full of information for another 230-odd years.

To return to something I said earlier in this chapter: don't panic. Established businesses are in a hugely powerful position. They are not all about to be blown away by nimble new dotcoms. They can be the true beneficiaries of all this. They have powerful, tangible assets on their side. They have established brands; they have relationships with their customers; they have proven business models; they have ways of talking to their customers.

Compare that to the average dotcom. They don't have a brand. They need to spend heavily on marketing to establish in people's minds the idea of what they do. They have to communicate their proposition to people who are sceptical about using the internet, and they need to do that without the benefit of having an established relationship with them. They have to stand out from an ever-increasing competitive crowd. They have to build services that really work, that can replicate or improve an entire offline experience without human intervention. They have to learn to handle customers that they may never see or talk to. They have to grow at massive speed. They have to spend on creating their business, finding a complete staff from nowhere, developing technology. And, on top of all this, they have to make enough profit to pay back the massive amounts of funding that have been pumped into most of them – and profit is something most of them are very far from seeing.

Look at what happened in early 2000. Internet-only stocks took a tumble on both sides of the Atlantic. British fashion e-tailer boo.com, one of the most generously-backed start-ups ever with funding of £130 million, went bust. The company spent heavily, and it couldn't begin to attract the sort of revenues it needed to justify that spending and start to move towards profitability.

Arguably dotcoms have had the best of it in the US, with its established culture of funding high-tech start-up businesses. Traditional players have so far struggled to match the internet players' nimbleness and speed of movement. But even there, a shakeout is starting to happen. The likes of CDNOW and Drkoop ran into trouble because their burn rate was too great, spending money faster than they could make it. The victory of the dotcoms may be illusory, or at least short-lived.

New-economy businesses themselves are well aware of this. They're not arrogant enough to think that they'll succeed merely be being new and small – well, most of them aren't, anyway. They're aware that traditional businesses enjoy some big advantages. Here's Brent Hoberman of lastminute.com again:

'The great thing that traditional businesses have is a monopoly of geography. Nobody is saying the people won't go into shops. If you're a car rental company, you have that real estate at the airport, and people come out of the airport and see you there and that's the place a lot of them will still go to rent their cars. No one can take that away from you.'

People still need things. If you produce something that can be transmitted digitally, you have an advantage. People's experience of your brand has everything to do with their experience of the product or service you give them. A tangible brand is a powerful brand.

The internet can do a lot of things, but it cannot become a product. In many cases, it cannot even become the delivery mechanism. If you create things, you have an in-built advantage over internet companies that don't create anything. The trick is to work out where value is created: why people use your product or service, what you give them that they consider worth paying for.

Ernesto Schmidt is managing director of online music site Peoplesound.com. The company takes bands which are not yet signed to a record label and gives some of their music away for free online. If people want more of the same sort of thing, either by the same band or on a compilation, Peoplesound will sell them a CD. It's a neat idea. But even Schmidt is keen to stress that being online, having a clever idea and being smart and nimble aren't enough in themselves for companies like his to be successful.

'The real winners on the internet will not be the ones that replace bricks and mortar retailers or whatever,' he comments. 'They'll be the ones that understand that the internet changes the way consumers and retailers interact. They'll be the ones with strong brands and original, differentiated content. The BBC, for example, which is one of the most traditional organizations you could think of, has been successful online because it has precisely those things.'

There are a number of the ingredients that make for a successful new-economy player. There are hurdles that established businesses have to overcome, and ways of thinking about their business that they have to make themselves go through. Over the following chapters, I'll describe some of the issues, challenges and problems that the companies mentioned in this chapter are facing, and try to understand what lessons they've learnt.

CHAPTER TWO

CUSTOMERS

A business begins and ends with its customers. Whether those customers are consumers or other businesses, they're the first thing that business needs to get right. Sounds obvious, but to see the way that a lot of British companies operate, you wouldn't know it.

Identifying a customer group, working out what they want, and then refining your offer to take account of what they tell you about what they want, all these things are at the heart of good business practice. If a business puts its products and services at the heart of what it does, and expects customers to follow, it will suffer. Customers have to come first.

This has always been true. But for years, companies have been able to get away with being product-focused rather than customer-focused. The internet will end all that. The internet puts customers in control of their relationships with businesses more than ever before. It makes companies listen to their customers, and to their prospective customers, find out what they want, and act on it.

As I mentioned earlier, traditional economies are based on resources – raw materials that are scarce.

Whoever controls those scarce raw materials is in a position to exploit them and generate wealth. But a lot of the raw materials of the internet economy are infinite. The ability of a computer to execute the same function again and again is virtually limitless, for example. Everyone has the ability to own the raw materials of economic prosperity. So the focus shifts from who controls the raw materials to who can best persuade people to consume their product.

While sellers controlled the buying process, they were able to get away with putting their products before their customers. A company could produce something, promote it to a particular customer group, and if it did that well, they would buy it. Now those customers can go online, interrogate every aspect of that company's offering, compare it directly with rival offerings, talk to each other about them, and make an infinitely more informed, measured decision than they ever could before. Customers can demand to interact with you whenever they want to. Your doors are never closed. You can no longer set your office hours. You have to be prepared to talk to your customer at whatever time they want, through whatever medium they want. And you're forced to listen to them, and react to their demands. You can't just offer them a product and invite them to take it or leave it, because if you're not listening to their requirements and refining what you do to suit them, you can bet that another company will be.

A whole industry has built up around the business of putting more power into the hands of customers. There are numerous ways in which people can compare the offerings of various suppliers. They include comparison shopping sites, which rank retailers according to price, delivery time, customer service or whatever, and other comparison engines, for instance for different financial services products; collaborative buying sites, where people arrange to buy items in a group, and the site negotiates a bulk discount on their behalf; business trading exchanges featuring multiple business-to-business suppliers, allowing customer and supplier alike to choose their ideal partners; and sites where consumers and businesses alike can specify what they want to buy, and companies can bid for their custom. The list is almost endless. A lot of the clever dotcom ideas over the last few years have been variations on this theme – they have been about empowering the customer. The customer is in charge, and the successful businesses of the future will be the ones that realize this.

The moves of companies like Procter & Gamble and Unilever towards providing services are an acknowledgement of this. The way in which the fmcg giants have traditionally done business has been about creating a product and then selling it to people. The product is at the centre, a great, monolithic centre from which the company fires out its marketing. The customers are seduced by the marketing, and buy the product. In the new model, these companies are starting to acknowledge that the way their customers interact with them is changing. No one wants to buy individual items online. Web sites about their brands are not interesting, and no one wants to go to them. Brands mean more to people than a box of soap powder or a tin of beans on a shelf, but the internet risks turning their brands into little more than that. In order to get close to people, to talk to them in their language and to find out what really makes them tick, what these companies need to offer is services. Hence myhome.com. Hence reflect.com. They're services which explicitly put the customer at the centre. It's a massive shift for these organizations.

For most companies, the nature of their customers won't change that much. They'll still be targeting approximately the same people they always did. In most cases, it's a relatively small group of people; sometimes they're consumers, and sometimes they're other businesses. The business-to-business internet market has been the focus of a lot of attention. A July 2000 report from research company Jupiter estimates that the online market for business-to-business services was currently worth $336 billion a year, rising to more than $6 trillion by 2005, close to 50 per cent of the entire market. It's there, as much as in the mass-market consumer space, that the really interesting fight for customers will take place.

Before a company even starts trying to address its customers, it needs to work out who they are. For an internet-only company, that in itself can be a big challenge. A lot of companies have suffered from a lack of focus: they try and appeal to everyone, and risk ending up appealing to no one.

Most established companies will have a better idea who their customers are. But it's worth bearing in mind that those customers may well have changed. There is often an opportunity to reach a broader market than before – perhaps a broader demographic profile, or a broader geographical one.

It's not even always something the company concerned aims for. Publisher Miller Freeman, for example, launched a web site called dotmusic (www.dotmusic.com) as a spin-off from *Music Week*, its music industry magazine. But the inside information on the music industry featured on the site proved to be popular with consumers, and without the company really trying, consumers came to make up the bulk of its users. The site was re-invented as a consumer destination, and is now the UK's leading music web site. It wasn't something the company had set out to do, but it happened, and the company was smart enough to react accordingly.

Expanding its range of customers is always a big step for a company to take, and the effects of international expansion can be particularly profound and unexpected. The internet is a global medium, you're likely to get people from outside the territories you already operate in wanting to use your service, and it can seem almost self-evident that you should be expanding the reach of what you do to talk to those new potential customers. But companies need to think carefully about what their attitude towards these people is. They're a new opportunity, certainly, but the cost of servicing them may be prohibitive, particularly for companies that trade in physical items which need delivering. And if a company has always operated in a single country, it will be culturally attuned to addressing its customers in a particular way. In other countries, that might be irrelevant or, in the worst case, illegal. If it does decide to address a global audience, it needs a web operation that works globally. That means different languages, different ways of structuring information, different values, balanced with a consistency and harmony of appearance and of content. It's a tough one to pull off.

When it decided to remove the charge to consumers for using its service, John Charcol was making a conscious decision to address a wider customer base than it had traditionally been able to reach through its retail operation. Paying several hundred pounds to use a mortgage broker had generally been the preserve of the relatively wealthy. That was fine – John Charcol set the cost of entry so that it discouraged people with low-value mortgages from using its service, because the commissions on those kinds of loans weren't high enough to make it economic to serve those people. Online, the cost of administering each customer is far, far lower, and so the free service is suddenly available to a far broader range of people, and a far greater spread of mortgage values. There's also a difference in the complexity of the sort of mortgages that go through the site, according to Toby Strauss, managing director of Charcol Online.

'Our customers online are very different from the traditional sort of John Charcol customer,' he says. 'Traditionally, our customers are people with very complex requirements, who need to ask a lot of questions. The site can't deal with that. The people who use the web site are much more interested in serving themselves. Only 10 per cent of our online custom has been cannibalized from existing channels. The rest is new custom. Obviously, it's that other 90 per cent that we're looking to grow.

'When we were planning to do it, and on the way in, there was a lot of sensitivity internally about cannibalization. We agreed that we'd monitor it closely, and so far it hasn't been a problem. It's still the case that the main John Charcol business is focusing on the more upmarket customers than Charcol Online.'

Jungle.com addresses several different customer groups, and has segmented its offering so it can talk to each of them separately. The company actually operates three different online businesses, all of them aimed at different groups of people, and all of them with different pricing policies. Jungle.com is the consumer bit and doesn't offer consumers discounts. JungleDirect is aimed at the SoHo (small office home office) and SME (small and medium-sized enterprise) market and offers discounts only on the basis of multiple orders. Corporate Direct is aimed at big businesses, and there everything is negotiable.

The company agrees to sell to big corporate clients at cost price plus a certain percentage. It then sets up an extranet for the client with specific details of that company's requirements, and the prices it's going to be charged – something that can be set up and configured in minutes by the salesman from a spreadsheet-like application. The extranet then learns from the customer's use of the site, creating favourites lists and prioritizing them according to what the client buys most regularly. At the time of writing, there were 512 such deals in place.

Around half of the company's revenue comes from consumers, and the other half from businesses. Founder Steve Bennett says he wants to increase the lucrative business component as time goes on. The consumer element of the company's customer base is moving from offline channels onto the internet more quickly than the business element; consumers seem happier to migrate across to buying online more quickly.

The company charges the same prices whether people buy online or speak to a salesman, but with an additional delivery charge if they take the human rather than the virtual route – an interesting attempt at differential pricing which may not stand the test of time. As Bennett says, inconsistent pricing policies confuse and can antagonize customers, who tend to catch onto them pretty quickly and force them to be changed. And Bennett is nothing if not open to change.

The internet can turn good customers into better customers by serving them better. It can also expand a company's customer base. In both cases, companies that use the internet to try to increase their custom need to be able to deal with that extra custom if it comes.

One if the great ironies of the internet is that while it forces companies to be more customer-centric, the general standard of customer service online is dreadful. Week after week, I and my colleagues at *Revolution* talk to people with businesses based on great ideas, with fantastic, innovative business models, staffed by intelligent and entrepreneurial people, with web sites that aren't very good. It's amazing how many companies have robust, sophisticated business ideas, grandiose plans to shift lazy incumbents from their market-leading positions and take over the world – then you try and use their service, and find that the interface is difficult to use; it's hard to get a response if you have a query; it doesn't keep in contact with you, send you offers and make you feel wanted; and as for personalization, or any attempt to understand you as an individual customer, forget it.

Businesses have spent millions of man-hours and

invested extraordinary sums of money in customer service, in making sure that the customer's experience of the company is always a good one. It's one area where internet companies still have a huge amount of catching up to do.

Every week, members of the team at the magazine try and buy items on the web for a section where we write up an online shopping experience. The results are nearly always disappointing. The most common sticking points are customer service, in particular how good the company is at answering questions; the buying path on the site, the actual business of going through the purchase process; and fulfilment, the dirty business of delivering goods to people, whether through the post or to the door.

It's been fashionable for a while to talk about the actual design and layout of web sites – the interface that constitutes the customer's experience of a site – as if it were a relatively trivial thing.

In part this is a backlash against an undue focus on the web site as the centre of a company's internet operations, as opposed to just one link in a complex business chain. The real meat of e-business has been held to be in customer relationship management, business process, logistics, systems integration, and all that other back-end stuff.

That's all very well, but if the web site is useless, not many people are going to visit it, and those who do will go away with a bad impression of the company that owns it. Someone's experience of an online product or service is influenced at the most basic level by their principal interface with the business that provides it, the web site. The reasons companies like Dell and Amazon have become such e-commerce success stories have a lot to do with the usability, the simplicity, the friendliness of their web sites.

The whole business of managing customer interaction online, of making web sites easy to use, efficient, elegant and attractive, is still an inexact science, to say the least. The web site has to replace everything that people usually do for a customer. It has to give the customer the option of being able to remove all that human interaction and do it all themselves online. It also has to give them the option of re-introducing that human element at any point, should they wish to do so.

You'll often hear people say that getting the actual web site right is the easy bit. It isn't. Getting a web site right is extremely difficult. This applies to companies across the board, right up to some of the best-known names around. In its first year, for example, during which the company became a byword for the burgeoning, vibrant British e-commerce scene, lastminute.com's web site was very difficult to navigate and to find what you wanted on it. It was built for around £20,000, it groaned under the weight of demand, and as the range of items and the complexity of the site grew, the information architecture became ever more tortuous. Similarly, getting around a lot of big-brand web sites is still like pulling teeth.

If you start by thinking of a web site as product packaging, then at the moment, most web sites are like really good products packaged in a brown hessian sack. Widen it out from packaging, because it's more than that: a web site can be the whole way your customer interacts with a company – it's their window on that company, the beginning and the end of their contact with it, what it has instead of people to talk to them. Most web sites are like a shop with no signage, no tills and no sales assistants. They're really good products sold by a sales force whose idea of a persuasive sell is to hide the product behind their backs. Or who ignore customers who try and buy from them, or collapse to the floor when spoken to and won't get up again. Or who prevent people wearing certain sorts of shoes from buying them – this is what you're doing if, for instance, your site only supports certain types of browser, or insists that people download certain software to use it.

When it comes to designing web sites, there's a balance to be struck between form and function. The more visual elements you put on a page, the more difficult it can become to navigate. You want your web site to look attractive, because that affects your brand. But if it's pretty to look at and impossible to get around, then the experience of using the site is a letdown, and your brand still suffers. Keeping the navigation simple isn't incompatible with making a site visually pleasing. What will make it difficult for some users is excessive use of technology, features like full-motion video that require software to be downloaded. They'll be irrelevant, and quite possibly annoying, to most users. If you're a lifestyle brand addressing a very fashionable and extremely techno-savvy audience who are likely to expect it of you and able to deal with the technology, then go ahead. Otherwise, think very carefully.

I write this in the full knowledge that it will date this book, because at some point BT will roll out ADSL, a technology which will mean widespread internet access at speeds which will make full-motion video and the like an everyday reality. And other technologies will come along which will improve the experience even further. Access to the internet is only going to get faster. Even when that does happen, though, not everyone will have it, and so it's important to make sure your site is accessible to everyone, even if with just a cut-down version for people with less sophisticated technology.

This is right at the heart of what makes a company successful on the internet. Great ideas are all very well, but a great web site is just as important. When the value and promise of internet ventures are being assessed, the majority of focus is on the idea: how the business model works and what chance that has of success. In reality, there are some far more mundane factors that have a bigger effect on the likelihood to succeed or fail of a particular company. People are at the heart of a business's success (see Chapter 3). So is the ability to execute well against an idea. Selling books online is not a particularly brilliant idea in itself; it's the execution that will decide the winners, whether they be Amazon.com, WHSmith Online, Barnes & Noble.com or BOL. A major part of that is customer service. Amazon, for example, has succeeded on this front so far: it's phenomenally easy to buy, and to repeat-buy, from the site. It's easy to find what you want; there are good recommendations, both by the site, based on your preferences, and by other users; the company gives its users targeted special offers; the site remembers all your details so you don't have to enter them again, making repeat buying trivially easy; and delivery is quick, efficient and has a low rate of returns. Amazon's justification for a high marketing spend and a high customer acquisition cost is that once it's got a customer, it keeps that customer and extracts maximum value from them.

Fulfilment is the other area where it regularly all falls down. The difficult business of actually getting items into people's hands has become an issue for more people than ever before. Retailers obviously have to deal with it, and find ways of getting items to people, rather than relying on customers always coming to shops. All sorts of other companies find themselves selling direct to consumers for the first time on the internet, and are also affected.

People are used to walking away from shops with what they've bought in their hands. Obvious point, but an important one. Why would someone want to wait several days for something to be delivered? If someone wants to buy something, they generally want it now, particularly if it's a heavily time-sensitive purchase like groceries. Walking away from a shop with your purchase is an essential part of the buying experience. Practicalities aside, online shopping can't match high-street shopping as an experience, particularly when it comes to items like, say, clothes, that people like to pick up and try on.

A lot of internet companies trumpet the fact that they don't hold stock, instead simply acting as facilitators, as one of the great efficiencies of their business. Online auction companies like eBay, for example, simply let people trade with each other, without goods ever passing through the facilitating company's hands. But it can also be true of retailers. Holding stock is expensive and cumbersome; much better if you can simply plug into wholesalers when an order comes in and get them to fulfil the order for you.

This is how Amazon made its name in the US, and explains why it originally set up shop practically next door to one of that country's biggest book wholesalers.

The problem with holding no, or minimal, stock is that it may lengthen delivery times. It also puts the company supplying the product to the consumer completely at the mercy of a third party. To a certain extent, that's going to happen anyway, if you're selling items off a web site. You'll usually end up relying either on the postal service, or on a delivery company of some sort.

The nature of delivery is changing. Items that would have been bought from shops in the past are now being delivered to the home. The most obvious example is groceries: home and workplace grocery shopping would never have taken off on anything like the same scale without the internet. New companies are doing the delivering. The business of providing everything from couriers to vans to end-to-end logistics services for internet operations has suddenly become very lucrative, and lots of new players have sprung up. Some of them are unusual. Dairies, for instance, with their fleets of refrigerated vans, which get used for only small amounts of each day, are starting to muscle in on the act.

Companies have to decide whether to hire delivery vans from one of these third parties or buy their own fleet. If a company owns vans, it can put its livery on the side and get the brand in people's faces. But buying and maintaining a delivery fleet is a very costly business, and it's only really practical for very large players. Even they may wonder whether it's worth the hassle.

It is the same with warehouses. Big players will

already have them. Other companies will either have to build them or hire some capacity in someone else's. Companies fulfilling orders into people's homes are going to have to employ expert picker-packers, particularly if they're in a market like groceries, where one banana can differ enormously from another next to it. Companies are going to have to be able to learn individual customers' preferences, and be absolutely certain that they know how to choose items correctly for each individual.

There are other interesting implications to this shift in buying patterns. More delivery vans will be on the streets – and less cars driving to shops. It could mean that companies partner with each other to make their delivery operations more efficient. It could also re-distribute traffic around the day. Most people aren't going to wait at home every time they want something delivered. Companies are going to be swamped with people wanting items delivered in the late evening. Already, in the US, double-door fridges are being installed in homes, with one of the doors external, so that grocery providers can unlock the external doors and drop off groceries without having to enter their customers' homes.

Increased remote ordering means that new points of collection are springing up: service stations, for example. Home delivery from web sites could even herald the rebirth of corner shops, which are well positioned to be the local point of collection.

Most companies have never delivered direct to their customers' doors before. The internet is prompting a lot of them to start doing so for the first time. Those companies have to work out where they're going to deliver from. This isn't as easy as it sounds. Setting up a warehouse or network of warehouses specifically to cater for home delivery looks obvious. Warehouses, though, don't come cheap. And if you're a company that already has a store-based retailing operation, it effectively means setting up a whole new distribution business, rather than using the one you already have.

For companies with no retail heritage, the choice is relatively easy: you have to fulfil orders from somewhere, so you need some sort of distribution base to do so. But some established retailers take a different view. Tesco, for example, has spent a lot of time and effort over the years building up a super-efficient logistics operation for its real-world business. Items are unloaded from lorries straight onto shelves; warehousing, either in the store or elsewhere, is kept to an absolute minimum. When it comes to fulfilling home delivery orders, the company was faced with a choice: build a whole new warehousing network from scratch, or stick with the distribution centres it already had in the shape of its stores.

Fulfilling orders from stores has its disadvantages. It means that, instead of staff picking goods from a central distribution centre, they have to go around the store and pick items off the shelves like a normal shopper, a pretty labour-intensive way of doing things. It also makes it difficult for the company to increase the total number of customers it serves from each store, one of the things the internet is very good at, because staff picking items off the shelves for home shopping clog up the store just as much as normal customers do. But Tesco took the view that it didn't want to re-invent the wheel when it already had a highly efficient logistics operation in place. So all of its home shopping fulfilment takes place through the stores.

Marks & Spencer takes the same view. The company puts the integration of its online and offline operations at the top of its priorities, so it's no surprise that it also uses its stores as distribution centres. In fact, where it can the company duplicates every aspect of its fulfilment operation from its existing business. As head of e-commerce Peter Robinson notes, it makes simple economic sense to do so.

'We already had a catalogue shopping arm, and so we used that capability to get us up and running. With that kind of thing, it's about seeing where in the business we can leverage the best things we already have. The infrastructure we had in place for the catalogue business gave us a number of good things. It gave us an ordering system, a sortation system, call-centre support, a packaging capability, and delivery infrastructure. So the decision to use those things was a fairly simple choice to make. Leveraging stuff from our existing business is a bit of a no-brainer for us.'

Where it isn't set up to do things itself, M&S outsources to third parties. The physical business of delivering items into people's homes falls into this category, and so the company's logistics and fulfilment operations are all outsourced.

Suddenly having to travel into people's home for the first time creates a new form of customer interaction. Home delivery may be a difficult one for retailers to square with a strategy which has seen them invest heavily in creating a well-branded in-store experience. It looks like they're losing control of the purchase, and losing an opportunity for interaction. But that's not necessarily the case. When it first started its online home shopping service four years ago, Tesco found that the most common reason for deliveries being late was that its delivery staff were being offered cups of tea by customers (at least, they claimed it was cups of tea). That's a rather higher level of customer interaction than the usual couple of cursory grunts exchanged by most of us with the individual working at the checkout.

My own personal experience of using Tesco's home shopping service has been that the delivery people are the best thing about it. They've been helpful and courteous, and given me a good feeling about the company, even if some of the food that's turned up hasn't. Home shopping could ironically end up bringing about a closer relationship between retailers and their customers. It's possible that that couple of minutes of human interaction with the delivery man could be worth more than the hour in a carefully-branded store that has had millions and millions spent on it.

People's tolerance of failure online is very low. Whereas in, say, a shop, a confused, uncertain or dissatisfied customer can find an individual and, in most cases, they can get their question answered or problem resolved fairly quickly, online they're denied that human interaction. The internet is actually less interactive than real people. Often, companies don't give their customers the option to pick up the phone and talk to someone. And businesses don't always have the option of picking up a phone and talking to their customers to put a problem right. It can be a confusing and isolating experience, and businesses should never forget that. Give people as much reassurance and as much signposting as you can – you can't put too much of an arm round their shoulder. Unless it's absolutely impossible to do so, give people the option of ringing you up, if not to buy over the phone, at least to clarify questions they have about the online buying process. The phone, in theory at least, gets answered more or less immediately. E-mail doesn't. Even the best internet operators won't commit to anything more ambitious than a response time of a couple of hours. And if someone wants to do something online, like buy from a web site, but they have a question they need to ask before doing so, they're not going to want to wait for hours for a reply. They will really want to phone.

It's not just the complaints, where companies actually need to communicate with their customers, that are problematical. It's also the minor difficulties, where the ball is in the customer's court. When most people have a small problem, they just walk away. It needs to be of a certain level of seriousness to get people, particularly British people, to take it up with a company. They're much more likely to do that in, say, a shop, where there's a person to talk to, than on a web site, where it can seem far too much like hard work to get a trivial query answered. That's why more than half of the time, when visitors to a site put items into a virtual shopping cart, they subsequently abandon it, rather than completing the purchase. People put items in them, but as soon as they run up against a brick wall, no matter how easy it would be to scale with a bit of help, they abort what they're doing.

Jungle.com has experienced all the challenges of online customer service in glorious technicolour. As you might expect from a company with a retail and mail order background as Software Warehouse, but an online future as jungle, the company has been trying to shift its customers onto the internet. According to managing director Steve Bennett, though, it won't be forcing the issue.

'People will still buy from people,' he comments. 'There will always be people who want to buy from another person, and we will continue to give them that option by phone. We want to give people every option except retail. But the whole way we'll get people working on the phone to work is to persuade customers to go back onto the web and buy there.

'We're migrating people onto the web because our customers get a better shopping experience that way. But there will always be a need for salespeople, particularly with computer products. At the extreme, you get super-techie people who ring up because they want to know the bus speed of a particular processor. You can't put things like the bus speed on the web site because you'd scare off 80 per cent of your potential customers if you went into too much technical detail. So you have to have people who can answer those kinds of questions.'

What took jungle.com by surprise, as Bennett freely confesses, is how labour-intensive the whole business of dealing with customers on the web can be. In fact, the company has had to increase its customer service operation since it embraced the internet as its primary sales channel. The company as a whole has grown by 20 per cent since the launch to cope with the unforeseen extra work.

'The customer service side of the business has actually grown a lot,' says Bennett. 'Almost everything in business becomes cheaper in the internet economy, but customer service becomes more expensive. The reason is that when people are phoning you, you tend to be able to resolve their problem first time. But if they send you an e-mail, it tends to go back and forward several times. We have ninety customer service people, and more of them are dealing with online enquiries than offline.'

The company uses intelligent software to send set responses to certain enquiries. The software looks for key words and phrases, and sends out what it thinks is an appropriate response. The pitfalls of letting a machine decide what response to send in a potentially sensitive customer service situation are obvious. Jungle.com employs someone to check that the responses are appropriate. 'Some companies use software totally automatically, but we don't want to risk that yet,' says Bennett. 'The software is 90 per cent of the way to getting it right every time, but we need it to be 100 per cent.'

It may look self-evident that customer service conversations conducted by e-mail are going to be more labour-intensive than those conducted by phone. But when it launched, jungle.com didn't foresee the strain on its customer service function at all. The company had spent a fortune advertising its launch, and the advertising apparently worked. Jungle was swamped. It generated eight million pages impressions in its first three days, and ended up selling more than a million items in the first month – its pre-launch target had been 300,000. The company simply couldn't get items out of its warehouses quick enough.

The result was a deluge of customer service enquiries, and the company couldn't handle it. It had underestimated how much e-mail correspondence it would be dealing with, and the customer service department was too small. At one point there were around 4,000 e-mails unanswered. The knock-on effect of this was complaints, about 600 of them in all. Bennett ended up suffering every business person's worst nightmare – being hauled up before that very smuggest champion of the British consumer: Anne Robinson on the BBC's *Watchdog*. Bennett insists that as a percentage of the company's total business the number of complaints, even in those problematic early days, has always actually been quite small. None the less, the *Watchdog* appearance resulted in the Consumers Association temporarily taking away from jungle.com its Which Web Trader kitemark, given to businesses that reach certain standards of customer service. 'The whole thing came as a complete shock,' admits Bennett. 'We got caught out.'

Jungle.com's mass-marketing campaign around the time of its launch was actually too effective. The company ended up getting caught on the hop, and there were two linked reasons for this: it wasn't expecting the level of custom it got; and it didn't realize how much resources were required to service each customer.

It sounds like a nice problem to have, and it meant that the company's sales volumes were extremely impressive. But it also meant that for a while, it had to struggle to regain its reputation. All the publicity it had received had identified it as a company with substandard online customer service, a nightmare for someone as proud of his customer service record as Bennett.

There's a broader lesson here. Getting as many customers as you can through your web site might seem uncontroversially a good thing. But if you're not set up to deal with them, it can be as disastrous as not getting enough. Marketing is one of the screws you can turn to control the number of customers you get; jungle.com turned it up to the max and found that it couldn't cope. Its problems may not have done its brand too much long-term harm, but it was a strain it didn't need early in its young life as an organization. And failing to meet its customers' expectations is about the worst crime any company can commit.

As Bennett points out, one possible answer is automation. If a business is flooded with requests from customers, and finds that when these come by e-mail they're actually more time-consuming to deal with than they used to be, it may turn to technology as a solution and use the sort of automated response software he describes.

Peter Robinson, head of e-commerce at M&S, is keen for this kind of automation to take over the bulk of responding to customer enquiries that the company has to do, because it's cheaper and more efficient than doing it manually. But he doesn't see it happening soon.

'E-mail customer service is growing rapidly. We're trying to cut down on the number of e-mails we have to physically send out. We have software which helps to assist in our customer response. We have the ultimate goal of responding to every query automatically, but we will have to grow the memory and the intelligence of the software for a while before we can do that, by feeding in the questions we receive and building up a greater range of answers. The complex questions will still inevitably need a person to answer them going forward for quite a long time.'

The danger with automation, of course, is getting it

wrong. Total automation can be dangerous, because a software program is not a person, and however sophisticated and intelligent it is, it won't always be able to interpret correctly each individual new customer query. And there's nothing more irritating to a consumer than receiving an obviously automated reply which doesn't answer their question. It doesn't get them any closer to resolving it, and it also has the unfortunate effect of making them feel that the company in question doesn't particularly regard them as an individual, or value their custom that highly.

Toby Strauss at Charcol Online argues that even if automated customer service software were to become 100 per cent reliable (something which isn't beyond the realms of possibility) it wouldn't necessarily be desirable to use it all the time. For him, the contact the company has with its customers when they ask questions is absolutely crucial. It's an opportunity to learn how customers are using the service, improve it according to their comments, and make them feel that the company values their opinion. In John Charcol's case, this is partly a function of the relatively small number of customers the company deals with, and its need to establish its trustworthiness with those people.

'In a way, we're lucky, in that ours is a low-volume, high-value transaction, so the sheer number of customers we have to deal with is quite small,' he explains. 'But people won't buy high-value items unless they trust the person they're buying from. We're lucky in that the process of administering a mortgage application is exactly the same online as offline. It's administration against a set process. But each customer service interaction is an opportunity, because getting some human contact with the customer is always a good thing. People want to be talked through the process. The received wisdom is that you keep iterating, you keep developing the self-service element of the site, until your customers never need to call you. But I think that however well you did that, you'd find that your conversion rate went down. It's important to get human contact.'

Strauss sees every customer interaction as an opportunity to improve what the site offers. Listening to even the most irate customers is at the heart of the way he wants the Charcol Online offer to develop.

'We have an escalation procedure for complaints, and some of them eventually find their way through to me. I find it really interesting. We have to listen to those complaints and learn from them. For example, we've rewritten some of the words of the site because they're misleading to some people. And we had a rash of people asking for us to have buy-to-let mortgages on the site, so we introduced a buy-to-let section. We can be more responsive to what people actually want.

'Usually, though, we find that people are complaining because they've got the numbers wrong.'

Technology needn't always make the business of customer interaction more remote, less human. Much of it is claimed by its manufacturers to improve the quality of the customer service experience, reintroducing a human element and providing sophisticated tools for talking a customer through a particular online experience, for instance by allowing someone in a call centre to see what a person using a site is seeing and guide them through it. These sorts of tools will undoubtedly become more widespread in the future, as they are pushed heavily by technology companies.

Peter Robinson at M&S is sceptical of technology like this, because it seems to remove some of the efficiencies that the company has been able to make online. 'There's a huge wave of people trying to sell things like web call centres and so on, where someone in a call centre takes over the customer's browser and helps them that way,' he comments. 'But while there isn't the scale, the cost of doing some of these things makes them a tough call. One of the advantages of e-commerce, of taking orders over the internet rather than through a call centre, is that it can remove some of the cost. If you start doing all these new customer service things, then you start reintroducing a shed-load of those costs.'

Chris Hall, Dell's internet business manager, backs up the view that the key to good customer service on the internet is flexibility, and giving people as many options as they need. But the company wants to push its customers in the direction of buying online wherever it can, because the advantages are so evident, both to the company and to its customers.

'We know that if people have visited one of our web sites, the number of calls they make to us is going to be less. It's not about us insisting that once a customer has used a web site, they have to go down the online route and that route only. But we give them that option, and we know that if they buy online they'll be a happier customer, because they'll receive better service levels. The error rate is lower online, and the order gets into the factory quicker. If you fax us, you decide on the layout and format of that fax, and so we have to interpret the fax when it arrives. If you fill in a form on the web site, that form will be in a set format, so we'll know exactly how to interpret it.

'On the service and support side, what we do has to be all about getting people to administer it themselves online. On the sales side, we have to be a bit more flexible. If a consumer says that they don't want to order now, but they might order in three months' time, well, the range might have changed then, so we push them towards the site. Throughout the entire consideration period, we let them do whatever they want. If they want to ring, we let them ring. We're not frightened to challenge our customers and get them to buy online, but we have to give them options.'

Dell sells to both consumers and the business community. Its customer base stretches right from an individual buying an entry-level PC through to some of the world's largest corporations. A company like Marconi, for example, buys a lot of its computer equipment from Dell's web site.

Dell serves all these different customer groups through the same site, which is divided into sections for each of them, such as home and home office, small business, large business, and public sector. Inevitably, it's easier to sell lower-value items online, because there is less likely to be a need for complex questions, and there is no bulk-buying and therefore no price negotiation. On the other hand, a lot of the IT buying of large organizations is a fairly mechanical business: much of what they're going to need is fairly predictable.

Dell builds special web sites for corporations that choose 'to engage wholeheartedly with us online', says Hall. He adds that because the company wants its customers to buy online wherever possible, again because of the cheaper administrative costs that brings, it has gone as far as reducing prices in order to give them a push in that direction. 'We have, in heavy negotiation, incentivized customers to buy online, and we've passed the cost-saving from them doing so on to them,' he says.

There's no doubt about it – acquiring customers is expensive. According to a survey by the Boston Consulting Group, internet-only companies in the US spent an average of $82 acquiring each customer in 1999. For companies that combined a web operation with an offline presence, the figure was a dramatically lower $12.

The cost of customer acquisition, and the value of each customer acquired, which needs to be offset against that cost, depend on a number of variables – largely the same ones as they would in the offline world. The main one is the market the company operates in. If it offers someone something very expensive, with a high profit margin, it can spend a lot of money trying to persuade a customer to buy it. Look at the automotive manufacturing industry, where companies can easily spend several thousand pounds on advertising and promotion for each vehicle they shift.

Another variable is how much customer inertia there is in a particular market. In financial services, say, and particularly in an area like banking, acquiring customers is expensive, because most stay with one provider for long periods of time. For exactly the same reason, customers have a high value once acquired, because they're less likely to move on, so it's worth spending more to acquire them. The game then becomes one of how good companies are at retaining customers once they've got them: on the internet, that means how good their customer service is, how tailored to their personal requirements they make the experience of using their services, how often they talk to them and foster their loyalty. A high cost of customer acquisition is only justified if they can then keep that customer at a relatively low cost. Cost of customer acquisition is high, but at least it's relatively easy to plot expenditure against number of customers acquired. Customer retention can also be an expensive and resource-intensive business, and it's a lot more difficult to track.

Established businesses have an advantage here. In most cases, they already have at least some of the customers they want to be addressing online. Getting them to use a different medium, if that's their aim, isn't too difficult – they know who they are, and all they need to do is address them in the right way with the online offer, and give them some kind of incentive to make the switch. Keeping them once they've made that switch is the interesting bit.

Finding new customers is easier for established business than for their pure-play online counterparts, too. They have an established brand name, a reputation, collateral on which to promote the new service (everything from bags to shopfronts to sales literature to letterhead), and so their cost of customer acquisition can be a lot lower. More of this in Chapter 5.

You'll hear a lot of talk in the internet space about lifetime customer value. The idea is that you can spend a lot to acquire a customer, because once you've done so, you've got them for life. The elegance and efficiency of the way in which you deal with them online will lure them into a lifelong cycle of convenience-driven repeat buying. Buying from you will be so simple that they will never want to go anywhere else. It's true only in so far as companies are effective at keeping their customers. There's no physical distance between you and your competitors online. All anyone has to do is write another web address into their browser to find an alternative. As I mentioned earlier in this chapter, comparing suppliers has never been easier. Customers are in control, and so they're more likely to move around and try to find the best deal. The real trick is working out which buttons to press in order to keep them.

That means talking to them when they want to be talked to. Because customers can interact with businesses online whenever they choose to, those businesses can box themselves into a purely reactive mindset. But if a business wants to keep customers when it's got them, and turn them into repeat customers, then it needs to keep talking to them. This is particularly true if a business has a complex, ever-changing product, which people want to keep up with (and here something like Charcol Online is again a prime example – requests for more information are the thing it gets asked for most often). People want contact from a company because they want to feel valued. They also want to keep up with what it can offer them.

When you're in that kind of relationship with your customers, one where they actually want information from you, your attitude towards customer communication needs to be considered carefully. Traditional direct marketing, for example, thinks of a response rate to a mailshot of 2 per cent as a success. That's because it anticipates a lot of wastage. To a greater or lesser extent, depending on the level of targeting, the message will be irrelevant to a certain number of the people that receive it. On the internet, if people have asked for information, then you're expecting higher response rates. Your communication ceases to be speculative, broad and general; it becomes proactive, demanded by the consumer, narrow and specific. People are unlikely to be so resistant to promotional messages if they feel they're getting something of value to them personally.

In order to give them that, companies need to find out about them. That means getting them to surrender data about themselves. In these days of ubiquitous loyalty programmes and saturation direct marketing, people are increasingly savvy about the value of data. They're not keen to tell companies all about themselves, something which can often be a time-consuming process, unless they feel they're getting something in return. That means providing an incentive to surrender information. Often, this takes the form of a competition or other promotional offer, in return for filling out a form, registering on a site, or providing some other form of information about themselves. One problem with this is that no one can be sure of people's motivation. They may just want something for nothing, and have no intention of becoming a customer. The best incentive anyone can offer them is some sort of service improvement; in other words, something which helps them to identify the people who really do want to use a product or service, and then helps the company providing it to tie them into a closer relationship.

Companies trying to identify their best customers and give them something extra need to go about constructing that list of people very carefully. Traditionally, direct marketers construct lists by asking people to opt out if they don't want to receive information on a company, typically by asking them to tick a box. If the box is left unticked, that individual is assumed to be interested in receiving the information, or at least not to have a violent aversion to doing so.

On the internet, it's usual to be more cautious, for companies to send information only to people who have actively specified that they actually want it. E-mail is an intrusive medium, and if a company uses it to communicate with customers it needs to make sure that they want it to do so. That's why list-broking – buying data off third parties – is frowned on. Unless someone has said that they want to receive information from a company then it shouldn't give it to them. Junk e-mail, otherwise known as spam, is one of the great curses of the internet. It's easy to hoover up e-mail addresses and send out irrelevant junk to millions of people, and so a lot of it gets sent. People spend a lot of time opening and deleting irrelevant offers, and in general, it annoys them. The very worst thing a company can do is to send e-mail which allows it to become associated with this kind of practice; its reputation can be damaged irreparably. More importantly, if it takes care in the way it assembles its list of people that it wants to keep in contact with, they'll be better prospects. There may be fewer of them, but if they're its top customers, that doesn't matter, it's worth spending more on talking to them. The internet is often as much about turning existing customers into better ones as it is about gaining new customers.

*

Once a company has gathered data about people, it needs to use it carefully. Associating data collected online and data collected offline is legally and ethically a dangerous business. Using data collected one way for a different purpose could breach the Data Protection Act, and the equivalent data legislation in other countries. It is something that not many online operators understand.

US company DoubleClick gathers data anonymously online and uses it to serve up relevant internet advertising to people. The company got in trouble when it bought direct marketing company Abacus Direct, which had a completely separate set of data, gathered offline. It meant the two data sets could be associated, and there was a danger that the profiles would no longer be anonymous, that the company would be able to put a name to each profile. It's a trap which companies can easily fall into, however inadvertently.

None the less, if a company has information about people, it needs to use it. If people hand over personal information, they do it in the expectation of getting something in return. Beware of falling into the trap of thinking of data as an end in itself. Getting data, a certain number of customer registrations, or whatever, is often spuriously used to judge a company's success on the internet. Ultimately, the only metric that matters is the amount of business a company does: the only figure it can use to gauge success or failure is the bottom line.

As a company knows more and more about people, the messages it sends out to them will need to become ever more tightly targeted. Just throwing the same single promotional e-mail in the direction of every customer once a week is missing out on the opportunity to provide something of relevance, and will just end up annoying them. The great goal of a lot of companies, and something which the internet accelerates, is talking to each customer as a separate individual.

There are a few problems with this, however. For a start, it's much more talked about than done. There are huge software and consultancy industries which have sprung up to tell people that they should be segmenting their customers down to the level of one-to-one, or as close to it as they can get. While this thinking and these tools have undoubtedly delivered a lot of benefits to companies, if you ask them for examples of companies that truly address each of their customers as an individual, and that successfully and automatically personalize those customers' online experiences, they'll struggle (and believe me, I've tried). It's a great opportunity, but phenomenally hard to pull off.

It's extremely complex, and that makes it expensive. Using the internet is generally regarded as a money-saver, it making the cost of administering customers much lower. But the more tightly companies segment their customers, the more messages they have to send out, and the more expensive it becomes. The personal touch costs money. And deploying highly complex pieces of personalization and customer relationship marketing software is expensive.

Besides, it's healthy to question how desirable true one-to-one communication with customers really is. Apart from the expense, there's the issue of how far people really want it. Undoubtedly they want more relevant, targeted communication from businesses, but full-scale one-to-one marketing? There's an element of Big Brother about it. Sometimes people crave anonymity. As for personalization, there are occasions when people want a choice. And if you're personalizing with software, you run the risk of getting it wrong. You can end up trying to second-guess people's preferences rather than letting them decide. So-called collaborative filtering, where people's interests and preferences are predicted by studying patterns among similar people, runs the risk of stereotyping people. You put them in boxes, and miss out on opportunities.

So while reducing the amount of irrelevant material customers are sent and making them into better customers with targeted communication has to be a good thing, tread carefully. Get it wrong, or take it too far, and you can lose touch with what it is that customers really want.

At the heart of every business are its customers. It is nothing without them. Pre-industrial businesses knew their customers. Industrial businesses found it hard to know their customers, but that didn't matter, because new efficiencies of production and distribution enabled them to reach numbers of customers that they could never have reached before. The danger for internet businesses is that they get trapped into the industrial way of thinking. It is increasingly difficult to simply create a product or service and expect people to come and use it. Long before the internet came along as a business tool, companies were trying to relearn their pre-industrial lessons and know their customers better, so that they could identify what it was that made their customers tick, find the best ones and build relationships with them. The internet makes those things easier, and makes it more imperative to do them. The successful businesses on the internet will be those that are focused on each customer as the epicentre of everything that they do as a company. What the customer demands, the customer gets.

CUSTOMERS

CHAPTER THREE

STAFF

Hoary old cliché alert: the success of any business is based on the quality of its people.

You're only as good as the people you hire to work for you, or with you. (Here we are talking about direct staff, those on the payroll; the question of outside suppliers is discussed in Chapter 6.) The fact is, when you're dealing with the internet you're going to find that all the people issues you've ever faced are magnified and intensified. In this economy, it's more difficult to decide what sort of people you need working for you; it's more difficult to find people who fit the bill; it's more difficult, once you've found them, to persuade them to come and work for you; and it's more difficult to keep them working for you for any length of time.

The internet blurs boundaries between what people do. In most companies, it was passed around a series of departments before anyone realized this. Generally the IT department got hold of it first. Most often they were followed by the marketing department. Hence the proliferation in the early days of the world wide web of brand communication web sites that did little more than say 'our company/product/ service is great – please come and interact with it. And then go away and buy it.' Not much use if your product is a can of baked beans or a spark plug. For low-interest, low-involvement brands, the internet isn't very good at brand communication in the traditional sense. You end up with very dull sites – what used to be known as brochureware.

It's an example of the way in which most companies' use of the internet refuses to correspond to particular, well-defined, existing disciplines or functions. You can't just recruit a load of technical people, or a load of marketing people, or even a load of business strategists, and hope that they'll be able to run your e-commerce operations. They won't have a broad enough skillset. It's better to look at what you actually plan to do with your online presence. If you're going to sell online, that's retail, so you need sales people, and people with retail experience. Except that selling online, particularly if your core business isn't retailing, may change the whole way in which you do business. In that case, you may need corporate strategy people, which could mean recruiting people with a consultancy background. And if, say, you're having to deliver direct to customers for the first time, and you're altering the way you take orders from suppliers, then you're going to have to get some pretty hot logistics people in as well. In other words, the internet is something that affects the whole of a business, and so the only place the decisions can come from is the very top. And the people at the top can't do everything themselves; they've got to find new people to make it work.

If you're a small business, you're faced with the

daunting task of finding a person or people who can cover all these bases. If you're a big corporate, you can employ a whole new team, but that doesn't mean you've got it much easier. Those people are going to have to work closely together and overlap in job functions all over the place.

It's easy to get lost searching for the mythical über-internet-strategy-operations-business-genius. Finding the right people is going to remain a nightmare for quite a while yet. It's a simple question of supply and demand. The internet economy is booming at an incredible rate, and the need for good people to do the newly-created jobs is always going to outstrip the supply of good people available to do them. New people are flooding into the pool of available labour, but they're inexperienced, so individually it's difficult to assess their worth. Meanwhile there's a small pool of people with some experience, who do have their feet on the ladder, chasing ever more lucrative jobs with new employers who are forced to pay more and more if they want to attract them for senior positions.

Almost no one has serious experience. In particular, people who have done the actual hands-dirty, operational business of running a company are extremely thin on the ground. There are lots of would-be strategists who can tell you what you ought to be doing, but are very unlikely to be able to do it for you. The strategic management consultancies, strategy firms and even big auditors are emptying of people who have all the experience in the world of telling other companies how they should run themselves and now figure that this is the first time in history that there's a chance for them to set up a company, put all those fantastic ideas into practice and get rich quick.

The problem that a lot of them are finding is that three ex-McKinsey consultants do not a company make. You need people who know how to manage a complex process, to motivate and manage people, and to manage ridiculous and unprecedented rates of corporate growth. Very few people working in the internet industry have that. So you may well be forced to look outside. You may well be forced to look outside your own industry as well.

As ever, finding people with transferable skills is more important than finding people with directly relevant experience. And as ever, finding people who fit into a company culturally is at least as important as finding people with the right skills.

Internet-only operators have the ability to create a culture from scratch, to deliberately set out to make themselves desirable working environments which attract exactly the sort of people they're looking for. It's an opportunity which, for the most part, they pass up. There's a sweatshop feel to quite a few start-ups, and many suffer from a shortage of inspiring leadership which can communicate the rewards of working there to employees and make it all seem worthwhile.

Established businesses have, or ought to have, structures in place for looking after staff. And, most importantly, they already have a work culture. They can change that when they create an internet division – and in fact more often than not they ought to, because they'll be looking for a different sort of person – but if they have a name and a history that means something to people, it makes their recruitment task immeasurably easier. There are benefits they can offer people, and cultural dimensions to their particular business they can dangle under their noses, which are likely to be a far more cost-effective hook to lure good staff than a big brick of cash. Big bricks of cash undoubtedly work in attracting people, but no one wants to go chucking them at people unless they absolutely have to, and there's always a suspicion that the sort of person who's motivated solely by money isn't going to make the best employee. If nothing else, they're likely to be off as soon as a higher offer comes along – and it will.

As you'd expect from the man who heads one of Britain's highest-profile dotcoms, Ernesto Schmidt at Peoplesound.com believes that traditional companies will struggle to compete with the new start-ups when it comes to attracting people. A former business strategy consultant, Schmidt sees this as a symptom of a broader malaise that affects established businesses: an inability to adapt to change quickly enough.

'The traditional ailment of established companies is that they are ossified organizations that can't move fast enough,' he says. 'In order to allow themselves to move faster, some traditional companies try to move the internet element of what they do out of house, but it always feels like a subsidiary, and it'll always affect the main company.

'The entire ethos of a dotcom is different. You've just got to "go go go". Traditional companies can't do that. It's very hard for an established company to justify the impact on its profit and loss of investing £30m a year on an internet venture.

'There are people perhaps three layers down the company who earn more than me. There are 23-year-olds on very high salaries, because they sit on a certain value, particularly technical people. The ossification of traditional companies, with their various levels of sign-off and their hierarchies of authority and pay, means that they're unable to recognize and reward that value.'

For example Peoplesound.com hired its marketing director, Mike Levine, from Procter & Gamble and, as highlighted earlier, that's about the most structured, ossified traditional company structure imaginable. Schmidt is adamant that just as the big, established players will not be able to compete with nimble start-ups when it comes to recruitment, neither will their businesses be able to adapt fast enough to the pace of online change to keep pace with the newcomers. 'If you look at a market like online share trading, why have the big investment banks been unable to replace the small online players, companies like e*trade?' he asks, a fire in his eyes. 'Why haven't [the US's biggest book retailer] Barnes & Noble been able to beat Amazon.com? It's because they're not comfortable with progressing and expanding.'

It's not all doom and gloom for the established players, however. As even Schmidt admits – and it would be hard to find a more committed apologist for the new economy – the speed of growth of internet companies, with their lack of trading history and established business process, makes them as vulnerable to the problems of over-rapid expansion as their online-only counterparts.

'Dotcoms have a problem too, but it's the opposite problem,' he admits. 'They tend to experience hyper-growth. They are organizations that risk choking on their own fluidity. The biggest managerial challenge within a dotcom is managing that. In October [1999] we found that we were incapable of managing that. It took the founders of the company to go back to the original plan and map out the business processes, in the way that people with a consulting background do, and it took a month and a half. My prediction for dotcoms being run by bright young things is that they will very soon have to get good project people to manage process across the whole company. It's absolutely vital that you employ good managers.'

Talk to people who recruit for internet companies for a living, and they'll tell you that you need to find cleverer ways of differentiating yourself as a potential employer. Here, for example, is Victoria Lubbock, managing director of one of the leading internet recruitment consultancies Recruit Media, quoted talking to *Revolution* (7 June 2000, p.29):

> There's a lot of hype about wages, and the whole business about paying excessively to attract people. It's very exciting that we're in an economy where people get to share in the wealth that they've helped to create. But the focus just on money is one-dimensional. People who are purely motivated by money will just wait until the next offer comes along.
>
> Yes, there are wage premiums to be paid, and certainly silly offers do happen, particularly when you're trying to employ strategy people, and technical people. But those offers are the exception. You don't have to do it that way. There are better ways for companies to make themselves attractive to work for, like family-friendly policies. Or structured training. Or flexible working hours.
>
> Everyone is offering options – they're all

offering something quite similar. It surprises me that people find it strange when we ask what the potential value of options is, or even the value of benefits. Just offering some options is not enough – you need to put a value on it.

The problem is that if companies accept it as par for the course that people will leave in six months, they don't know why they should bother putting good recruitment practices and attractive policies towards staff in place.

Lubbock is not alone in seeing this as a symptom of a wider malaise, and one that springs directly from the massive time pressure that internet company bosses inevitably find themselves under. 'The problem internet companies often have is an inability to communicate the vision of a business. They don't sell their company as a potential employer, especially the dotcoms. With established companies, at least employees know what they'll be getting. They've got a history – a culture is established.'

The received wisdom is that established companies, with their fixed, rigid structures, will never be able to compete for people effectively against the nimble, cash-rich, culturally-dynamic new players, where people feel part of a well-defined unit that has very definite aims and rewards. But they may not have to compete on those terms. If they have an established culture in place, one which people can see for themselves and which is effectively communicated by management to the rest of the staff, then they may have something very different, but equally valuable, to offer potential employees.

It is well known that people working on internet-related projects are now paid a lot of money. In particular, people with certain technical, project management and business strategy skills are able to command head-turning salaries, and the personal capital of those with serious internet experience rises all the time.

But a lot of the talk about internet pay is exaggerated. It's a natural human instinct to lie about what you earn, and the internet, with its lack of ground rules and bedded-down salary expectations for particular jobs, is the perfect place for people to claim that they earn a bit more than they do. With job mobility the norm, and some (although by no means most) people changing jobs every few months, there's an extra incentive to bump up your salary by a few grand when talking to a prospective new employer. It's easy to forget that in the storm of hype about 19-year-old dotcom millionaires, the majority of people don't earn that much more than they would for the equivalent job outside the internet economy, if they earn any more at all.

There's also a common misunderstanding about the nature and value of employee stock options or equity. Paper wealth is talked about as if it were real money, rather than a nominal value which may possibly be converted into cash in a few years' time – if the company retains its current valuation, goes public or is sold, and the employee then remains working for it for however many more years they're locked into doing so. A route to easy riches it is not.

None the less, with wage expectations so variable, particularly for the new roles that the internet throws up, in areas like business strategy, project management and programming, people will tend to ask for a lot.

And with good staff thin on the ground, quite often they'll get it. It's tempting, when looking for that elusive perfect person, to chuck a load of money, and possibly the much-loved options (if you're in a position to offer them) in the direction of someone who seems to have all the relevant skills. In reality, it's worth taking a deep breath and thinking about it before actually doing so. Could someone with less directly relevant experience actually do the job better – and more cheaply?

Toby Strauss at Charcol Online warns that it's easy to be sucked into the trap of trying to compete for staff directly with lavishly-funded internet-only companies by just pouring even more money into employee salaries. He sells his business as an attractive working environment, not as a quick route to easy money.

'We haven't had too much trouble attracting people to the business – a lot of our people come out of the big firms like Andersen's, and it's not exactly a difficult sell for us to those people,' he comments. 'But whether we'll be able to keep the people we've recruited is questionable. People tend to move on quickly because they get offered so much money. A lot of the dotcoms are trying to persuade people by paying them ridiculous wages which, in a lot of cases, they simply don't have to. I'd like to know if there's an inverse correlation between the size of the wages they pay and their chances of success.'

By contrast, Ernesto Schmidt at Peoplesound.com believes that people with the right technical expertise are by far the most difficult to find and hire. Like most, he's of the opinion that while skills are important, the cultural fit of an individual within an organization is much more important. 'The ideal hire for a company like ours is someone who has a skill within a market, and who also buys into the idea, who feels elevated when the idea does well,' he says. 'We need to have people who adapt, who are very comfortable with fluidity. If someone has exactly the right skills, but wants a written-down job description of exactly what they will be doing, they're no good for us.

'Everyone from traditional industries wants to move into an internet company and get stock options right now, so we don't have too much problem finding most of the types of people that we need. We can easily find marketing people, people from within the music industry, and whatever. But it's very difficult to find technical people, for example, because to have the necessary skills, they will tend to come from within the internet industry itself, and this is such a nascent industry that there aren't many of those people around.

'Good ideas are a dime a dozen. Getting the money is pretty difficult. But making it work is the bit that's really difficult, and that's a people issue.'

The classic example of a dotcom overpaying its staff was the now-defunct British internet start-up boo.com.

The company was comfortably the most generously funded internet start-up in Europe ever. It raised around £130m from various investors, including several Saudi Arabian backers; 21 Investimenti, the investment fund set up by the Benetton family; luxury goods company LMVH; Goldman Sachs; Bain Capital; and Sedco. The idea of the company was to sell sports and streetwear from fashionable designer names through an equally trendy web site. The plan was to launch in eighteen countries simultaneously in

May 1999. But a combination of technology problems meant that it didn't manage to get off the ground until more than five months later. This, combined with a lot of high-profile and very expensive advertising, much of which happened before the site had even launched, was the beginning of a downward spiral for the company. It quickly became something of a laughing stock within the internet industry. Its profligacy was legendary. The wasted advertising spend, the high salaries, the expensive offices, the phenomenally ambitious plan to trade across so many countries, the cost of the technology – it all escalated until boo imploded under its own weight. By May 2000 it had run through its money and its backers were getting twitchy. The company was burning up money at a fearsome rate, with no sign that it was able to halt the slide, and so one by one, they started to pull out. Soon after, the company went into liquidation. Management shortcomings, in particular a lack of financial control, were at the heart of its collapse.

One of the areas where the company's profligacy was most obvious was in its staffing policy. When the company was set up in 1999, we all gasped at the laudable ambition of a business which had several hundred employees before it had even started trading. At one point, the company had 500 people working for it. It even had its own online lifestyle magazine called *boom*, which wasn't even used as a promotional vehicle to sell the products available on the site. A collection of journalists were employed who were generously paid for working on a totally non-core activity, with extremely dubious value to the company's bottom line; it sucked away cash. Tales abounded of boo's employees taking first-class flights around the globe and staying in five-star hotels. The salaries they were paid, and the accompanying benefits packages, succeeded in getting a lot of people to come and work for the company. The problem was that they were also an awe-inspiring drain on the finances, one which couldn't be borne while boo was failing to make anything resembling revenues that would allow it to continue trading without further outside investment, let alone make anything so old-economy as profits. And while the company could cut costs by, say, losing a big chunk of its marketing spend, people are a lot more difficult to get rid of.

The overstaffing of boo.com, and the overpayment of the staff, were, in essence, a failure by the company's management to scale growth successfully. Most companies in their internet economy are surprised by the speed of their own growth. Even if they anticipate it, recruiting enough of the right people, keeping reporting lines consistent and retaining a coherent corporate culture are a big challenge for everyone. The danger is that you won't have the staff to cope with expansion. Boo over-compensated for this possibility. The company took the view that it was inevitably destined to grow at an accelerated speed, and that it should therefore recruit in advance enough people to cope with its projected future size. After all, it was a fantastically well-funded internet company with ubiquitous advertising, top-notch technology and a whizz-bang site – wasn't it inevitable that it would take over the world? The problem was that by rejecting the notion that it could grow organically, as demand dictated, it ended up exceeding what were reasonable costs for that business at that time. You can see why the company did it: it thought it was getting ahead of the game, and in some ways it was. The problem with boo.com was that it seemed to take the view that because it had a lot of money, it could therefore just go and spend it, in whatever ways and whatever quantities it wanted to.

The real problem, of course, was that the business wasn't very successful; its turnover didn't undergo the kind of mega-surge that would have supported its staffing levels and salaries. If it had been able to shift more goods, it would at least have been able to support its own weight, even if weaknesses elsewhere might well have brought it down eventually anyway.

For Encyclopaedia Britannica, the personnel shake-up has been profound, and in the light of subsequent developments, some of its staffing decisions now strike an ironic note. In 1998, the company got rid of its door-to-door sales force as a reaction to the fact that most of its revenue had started to come from sales of CD-Roms rather than books. Since then, as the company has tried to re-invent itself as a provider of internet-based content with a totally different business model, it has trimmed some old staff, attracted new ones, and faced all the staffing issues you'd expect when a company tries to change everything it does virtually overnight.

'We used to have seven thousand employees in the UK,' said Britannica.co.uk managing director Jason Plent when we met. 'We now have between four and five hundred. We got rid of the salesmen, and we also got rid of the logistics people, and the warehouse managers, and all those other people that were involved in producing, selling and delivering huge books to people. But although we now have a tiny staff compared to what we used to have, we employ twice as many editorial people as we used to, and twice as many technical people. The people that create the real value within the organization we now have more of.'

Brave words, but ones that struck an ironic note a couple of months later, when the company announced that it was slashing its UK staff.

As with any established organization without the in-built dotcom cool of a start-up, finding the right people was a challenge for Britannica. The company was in a better position to attract internet staff than it had been in its previous incarnation based on book publishing, but it was still saddled with a brand that the bright young things of the new economy wouldn't necessarily view as desirable to work for. But far from wanting to change Britannica to make it attractive to a different sort of prospective employee, Plent was adamant that the best way to recruit the best and most appropriate people is to believe in what you do as a company and communicate that well. 'Be in the business you're in,' he says. 'Don't try and, I don't know, change from being a distiller to a provider of football information, like some companies have done. Be in the business you're in, be proud of what you do and evangelize – communicate your enthusiasm for what you do. All the people here came on board because they saw the message we were sending out. It's difficult for us to be sexy, and we don't want to be, in a way, but that doesn't mean we don't want to inspire people.

'The principles we've established for running a business over 232 years still hold. The customer service director has been doing his job for twenty years, and he's got a 200-year legacy to draw on. You say to people like that: "Do the same as you've been doing, but do it through a different medium." The only way we built value in the first place was to take care of our customers, and we'll continue to do that online.'

The new company has an entirely different culture from the old one, and the transition to a new-economy way of working is something Plent is evidently proud of. 'I think it's really interesting, and it's been a real success, how the change in culture has been managed. As I say, there are people here who've been with the company for twenty years, and there's also a new team that has been brought together for the web development. But we've tried to keep hold of the people who do the indexing, who do the editing, who have the contact with academics. There's been a careful balance struck between the core skills which we needed to move across, and the new skills that we needed to attract.'

Perhaps the change of culture is best summed up by the change in the company's physical location. It has moved from decidedly unsexy Sutton to the heart of London's medialand, Golden Square in Soho, where it is surrounded by media companies and advertising agencies. And the people in the Britannica offices are not the besuited old bookworms you might expect. In fact, the make-up is not a million miles away from that of an internet development agency, or even, whisper it, a dotcom. As Plent says, the physical distance the company has travelled is an indication of the culture distance it has had to cover at the same time. Perhaps, in the light of the axing of britannica.co.uk and the company's decision to shed a third of its workforce, that distance was just a bit too far.

*

The process of recruiting staff for an internet operation isn't wholly one of shipping out existing employees and getting a load of internet whizzes in their place, with the inevitable reduction in average staff age to about twenty years. The internet isn't solely the preserve of MBA students, and companies shouldn't make the assumption that they have to get rid of everyone with a couple of grey hairs on their head.

The people with the grey hairs, experienced as they are at running a business, might just be your greatest asset. They're likely to have had more experience of the industry you're in, but more importantly they, and other experienced people from outside the company, know how to run a business. They can manage people, they can manage process, and they can manage growth. And they're much more likely to be taken seriously in deal-making situations.

Even companies that haven't historically had too many grey-hairs are starting to see the light and trying to recruit older staff. When Software Warehouse was a high-street and mail order vendor of computer-related products, it was mostly staffed and run by fresh-faced twenty- and thirty-somethings. However, as the company has morphed into internet retailer jungle.com, founder Steve Bennett has actually gone out of his way to recruit older board members. The prevailing ageist culture of the new economy isn't a given; some companies are heading in exactly the opposite direction.

'Our growth was slowing 1998-99,' he says. 'I knew I had to do something to change the business around, so I did something I'd never done before: I went out and bought a really good board of directors.'

That board consisted of experienced people with a serious business background. The company's chief financial officer Bob Jones, for example, previously held a similar role at mail order giant Empire Stores. 'I'm a bit of a bighead, and I always think I know everything,' comments Bennett. 'I thought I knew everything there was to know about mail order. But he's taught me a lot I hadn't even thought of, and given me new ways of looking at things.

'If you just employ young internet people, you get a lot of enthusiasm, but not much else. And all enthusiasm with no experience can lead to hyper-growth, but it also leads to big losses. You need to get people around you who'll challenge you, who know more than you do about certain things. It's like when you play sport: I'll never play squash against anyone who isn't better than me. What's the point? What do I learn?'

Non-executive directors play an important role here for the dotcoms. They don't have to employ heavy-hitters from a traditional business background full-time, but it helps to have some on the board. So lastminute.com has people with years of experience in the airline and hotel industries among its non-executive directors. For established companies, this shouldn't be a problem, because they should already have people with years of experience of their particular market working for them.

One way of staffing an internet venture is to move people around internally – take people who know the business inside-out because they already work there and move them onto the internet side. Companies trying to do this now at least won't face the problem that they would have faced a couple of years ago of no one wanting to do it. Now, everyone wants to be an internet guru. They're likely to risk alienating people who get left behind, though. In particular, they'll have problems with those people's direct managers.

Toby Strauss at Charcol Online recruited part of his team from the existing John Charcol business, but has also looked outside. A number of his staff have little obviously relevant experience, but he has taken the view that when it comes to staffing organization transferable skills are the key. Indeed, Strauss himself comes from a consultancy background. He wasn't previously an internet person, nor even particularly a financial services person; what he could do was manage people and operations. The same is true of the directors he's recruited.

'We've erred on the side of recruiting people of high quality who don't necessarily have that much relevant experience,' he says. 'We took our IT director from Andersen's. He doesn't actually have any experience of web development, but compared to the massive project management tasks he's used to, web development is actually quite trivial.'

Strauss was selective about which people he took from the main John Charcol business, partly because of the political ramifications of wholesale pilfering from a parent company. 'A few key people came across, like my head of operations and my head of product development,' he says. 'We also took some of the product development team from the existing business.

'The problem is that the main business is very resource-constrained, in exactly the same way as we are, and so we couldn't take too many of their people. But they recognized that there were people there with skills, particularly in areas like product development, who could help us. They're short themselves of people in areas like business development and IT, and it wasn't clear with those jobs that the insight they'd got from already having worked inside John Charcol would be particularly valuable to us. We didn't take people where we didn't think their experience of the company would be relevant. There are some areas where the experience of having worked for John Charcol would arguably be negative, because they'd be ingrained in certain ways of doing things.

'There are politics when you take people internally, of course. The operations side of the existing business was suffering anyway, and taking their deputy head to be our head of operations could have been a problem. We try to avoid wholesale poaching, because that would really piss people off. Fortunately we're not really big enough at the moment to make a big hole in the established business.' This is an issue of timing as much as anything, because sooner or later, Charcol Online almost certainly will be as big as its offline cousin, at which point both parts of the organization will face a difficult decision.

'Our requirements are different. We took a sales guy from John Charcol to be one of our technical people. He wasn't a particularly great sales person, but he was very thorough. And online, he doesn't need to be a particularly good sales person, because people who go to the web site are already interested, and they're pretty much going to sell to themselves – but his thoroughness is invaluable. The message is that people who weren't necessarily stars in the main business have flourished here.'

In exactly the same way as the internet cruelly exposes the weaknesses of existing businesses, so it has exposed John Charcol staff who don't do their jobs as well as they could, according to Strauss. 'The new businesses highlighted the weaker sales people to the main business – those who effectively charge for access to the exclusive products that we offer, rather than for the advice they give to customers. We're not in the business of being a gatekeeper to exclusive products and charging people to access them, and sales people who do that are starting to lose out because people can now access them online without a sales person.'

Even if a company doesn't take staff or other resources away from established parts of its business, it is still likely to come up against internal resentment. The very process of creating an internet capability within a company is going to tread on people's toes. There will be a general resentment from people who have been doing a job for years that what they do is by definition being devalued and implicitly criticized by the introduction of what is often a new way of doing the same thing. And if an internet division is set up as a stand-alone department within an organization, it's likely to be taking parts of their job responsibility away from them. If they work in the marketing department, and the e-commerce division has a separate marketing function within it, they can't help but feel that they're losing part of their empire. Making sure existing employees don't feel that they're being cut out, and giving them a role in making the internet work for the business as a whole, is one of the biggest challenges companies face.

When Dell took a conscious decision to put the internet at the heart of its business, it gave itself a staff motivation headache. The internet is a direct selling medium, where customers can self-administer: they can decide what they want, configure the sort of PC they're interested in buying and effectively serve themselves, there and then. That would appear to lessen the need for salesmen. So the decision to wholeheartedly embrace the internet as a sales channel had to put doubts in the minds of its sales force. Chris Hall, the man in charge of Dell's e-commerce operations in the UK, explains that the company got round this in a number of ways. The financial buoyancy and rapid expansion of the company at the time helped, but it was augmented by a conscious programme of education, planned from the very top.

'There were certainly sales people who feared for their jobs,' he says, 'but we're growing so fast that there's not been any loss of jobs. But more importantly, we trained all our staff in all this very early on. We actively encourage people to use the internet internally.

'The real challenge we had was embedding the internet in management objectives across the company, especially in the sales department. It's about getting people to think: "I know that getting people to use and buy from our web site is a company objective, but it's my objective as well." We've had to restructure the way we assess people's performance to reflect that. We had a bit of a rocky ride with some senior sales staff. Now we have success stories among the sales people, where there were nightmare clients and doing things online made that sales person's life a lot easier. What I say to sales staff is: "Each day, you only have maybe fifteen, or at most thirty minutes on the phone to each client. How do you want to use that time?" It's very important that the administration side of it is done by clients themselves. Then our sales staff can spend the time that they're actually talking to them selling, or doing the high-quality customer service stuff. It's also better for the customers – it's easier for them. It shows that the internet can genuinely be a win-win.'

The structure of the company reflects the fact that the internet is embedded into everything Dell does. There are separate, dedicated internet teams, but the internet is also a part of everyone's job across the company. There's a centralized web development team for the whole of Europe, which is linked in with all the company's other centralized European operations, such as its main factory and main call centres. There are also regional web development teams, staffed with both technical and business people whose jobs are internet-specific. Hall heads up all of those development teams across Europe. The internet is integrated into the business at every level.

For an organization like Procter & Gamble, the whole issue of getting the right staff for an internet venture is particularly tough, possibly more so for P&G than for any other company in the world. To understand why, you have to get to grips with the unique, and, to the outsider, quite bizarre culture of the company. P&G tends not to recruit people who have worked anywhere else. It is an extensive recruiter on the university milkround, taking bright graduates and training (some would say brainwashing) them in the P&G way. It leads to a loyal workforce; it is also, in theory, fiercely meritocratic – if people are any good, they'll be promoted if they stick around, and promoted relatively young by the standards of a big multinational. As long as the flow of people out of the company doesn't start to become a gush, and as long as the company choose the right graduates to employ in the first place, it is ensured a good supply of relatively cheap, enthusiastic, loyal managers. The problem is that with the arrival of the internet, the trickle of people leaving the company has become a flood. That makes finding the right people to take on the company's internal internet operations pretty challenging.

'P&G is being drained of people by the dotcom companies,' says the company's former European interactive boss Frederic Colas. 'Maybe not to the same extent as someone like McKinsey, but it's still a big issue. At the moment, P&G doesn't recruit from outside the company, but it's my opinion that this will have to change. A proportion of the people who are leaving will want to come back, in two, or three, or four years' time, when the dotcom fever dies down. Considering the experience and expertise they will have then, I believe that it would be a fundamental mistake to stop them.'

People in charge of any internet venture must decide whether they want to split their internet operations off as a separate department or try to integrate them with everything else that they do. A lot of companies have chosen to set up a separate internet division. It will be able to work faster and more independently than the main organization. It can also be funded separately if necessary, and be given more investment than its turnover would seem to merit by traditional business standards. And if it's successful, it can be spun off, or even floated separately, as Dixons did with Freeserve.

The disadvantage of a separate division is that

what you gain in speed and nimbleness, you lose in integration and communication. An internet division is something ghettoized, split off from the rest of the organization. The danger is that the two won't talk to each other, or will even start to regard each other as rivals. An established business ought to be a strength: it will have knowledge of its market, a brand, a customer base, established business relationships, and so on. If it fails to integrate its internet operations it risks losing all those things when it tries to do business online.

Peter Robinson says Marks & Spencer is keenly aware of both the advantages and the drawbacks of both approaches, and has tried to strike a balance between the two, while keeping the emphasis on integrating its internet activities into the main business. The company has a dedicated e-commerce department, which he heads, employing around twenty people. But more than 100 people across the organization have some kind of hands-on involvement in the company's internet trading activities.

According to Robinson, it's about making the most of existing resources, but introducing specialist expertise where it is relevant to do so. 'The objective of the e-commerce department is only to do things that the company doesn't already have in other parts of the business,' he says. 'So it has nothing to do with creating or sourcing product, for example, because the company already has that and is already very good at it.'

As head of the company's e-commerce operations, Robinson reports directly to the director of its direct selling division, but the e-commerce department operates independently, with its own budgets and targets. The appointment of Robinson as head of the new division is classic M&S strategy. Rather than bringing in some hotshot from outside who knew nothing about the company's business, it appointed an internet chief with nineteen years' experience at the company, who has done sixteen different jobs, covering everything from sales management for the foods division to store management. It is a sign of how highly the company prioritizes integrating the internet; more than anything else, what it wants is an e-commerce department which is sympathetic to the goals of the overall business.

Once you've got good people, you've got to keep them. There's a relatively small pool of experienced and talented people in the internet industry, and that doesn't tend to encourage employees to stick around for a long time at any particular job. In fact, most of the people I speak to are pretty miffed if they don't hear from at least a few headhunters every week. The problem is the recruitment mindset that says: 'We need someone to do a job for a company. OK then – what is that company's nearest competitor, and who is doing the same job there? Let's poach them and give them a big pay rise to do the same thing.' The result is people doing the same sort of job for more money, a stagnant labour pool with rising costs, and employees always on the lookout for their next move.

As Frederic Colas points out, there's a tendency for people working with the internet to have an inflated sense of their own worth, and for the expectations to rise constantly.

'A lot of people are leaving traditional companies because they find the internet fascinating, and because they want to be a millionaire,' he says. 'But whether they become one or not is a lottery. And the problem is that in a lottery, no one talks about the losers.'

If internet people are constantly offered new jobs, then companies need to do something clever to keep hold of them. The classic way is with equity or stock options. If they want to profit from them, people have to remain at the company for a given length of time because they can't sell their shares for a certain period, and having your financial well-being intimately intertwined with that of the company is a piquant motivator. Lastminute.com, for example, gives every single member of staff that it recruits an equity stake in the company.

'It's so obvious,' says co-founder Brent Hoberman. 'What you need to do is simply hire great people. Martha [Lane Fox, Hoberman's business partner] and I focus on what we're good at. What we're doing is selling all the time, selling the vision – and it's an exciting vision.

'We can also give people the salaries we need to give them to attract the calibre of people we need, and options to everyone. Existing businesses can't do that – if they do, they'll face a problem with cannibalization of salaries. And how can they attract good e-commerce people if they don't give them good e-commerce packages?'

As Hoberman points out, whereas a new company can give shares to a valued staff member fairly easily, not all traditional corporate structures can accommodate that kind of thing. If nothing else, it's a fantastic way to breed resentment among other staff members of equivalent or greater seniority, who have worked for the company for years, delivered a lot of value, but don't get the same financial privileges as someone much younger who just happens to have .com after their name. It's one explanation for the popularity of the spin-off: Tesco's decision to create a new company, Tesco.com, to take care of its internet operations, for example; or the Prudential's decision to launch its online banking enterprise, egg, as a separate company. If you create a new company, you can be a lot more flexible in the packages you give employees. The bottom line is that if you can't match the sort of deals the dotcoms are handing out, you're going to struggle to attract – and keep – the best people.

With the pressure of moving a business forward at hyper-speed, thorough and exacting recruitment procedures are one of the first things to go out of the window. In any organization, the most important part of recruitment is finding someone with the right cultural fit. The problem with over-hasty recruiting is that you can end up focusing too much on what skills they have, rather than the sort of person they are. Just ticking a series of boxes is not a qualitative way of recruiting. It's not only the enforced haste with which internet companies have to recruit that causes this to happen, it's also the fact that within rapidly expanding organizations, lines of authority and responsibility become blurred, and it can be hard to know who should be doing the recruiting. They're exactly the kind of circumstances in which recruiting can get delegated to someone who has no real understanding of the process and of how to select the right sort of person.

The opposite problem is a failure to delegate at all

by people at the top. This is something which particularly afflicts entrepreneurs; understandably, they see a company as their baby, and want to have complete control over who works for it. The problem is that people at the top of organizations, whether they be start-ups or established businesses, are highly time-pressured. They're not in a position to go through a thorough and diligent recruitment process, either. Recruitment consultants say that all too often, internet companies want nothing more than a brief CV with a list of skills and achievements. They're not prepared to put in time to find the right person. And if businesses are built on their people, and high-growth internet business in particular, then this has to be a dangerously short-sighted attitude.

Growth at extreme speed is difficult to manage. Finding the right staff is only part of the challenge. If your internet operations are expanding at an exponential rate, the biggest problem can be keeping a lid on that expansion and keeping a coherent sense of what the business does and who does what within it. It is possible to grow too quickly. There's no absolute speed that can be defined as too fast; the speed at which an organization grows depends on that organization, its people, the business it's in, the competitive landscape, and a whole host of other factors. It also depends on how well that company's management handles growth, how it manages scale.

There are several problems rapid growth can bring. One is cashflow: an organization's cost base will rise quickly, and its revenue will take a while to catch up. Other problems are infrastructural, as simple as how to find office space. I've spoken to people from internet companies that have carefully planned an office move because they were expanding so fast, selected new premises which could accommodate a far larger number of people, and then found, the day they moved, that it was already full to capacity. Time to start planning for the next move.

Just as the proliferation of adverts for internet companies has allowed media companies to charge more for advertising, because demand outstrips supply, so the burst of economic activity surrounding the internet economy has given rise to a need for more office space. That pushes prices up, and forces companies to look further afield than they would normally consider. New business areas have sprung up as previously unregarded inner-city areas and out-of-town sites have become the most practical and affordable options. London's Clerkenwell and Shore-ditch, the business parks around Cambridge, and the so-called Silicon Glen near Edinburgh are prime examples.

The decision to locate in an area like this is one pure-play internet start-ups can easily make if they think it appropriate to do so. For the internet divisions of traditional businesses, the decision is not so simple. Most would rather keep their internet operations as integrated as possible, which usually means locating it in the same building. However, with the pace of growth this isn't always possible. Separate locations can help breed a new company culture; but they can also damage communication between different parts of the organization, and create a mindset where they're as interested in battling with each other as in competing with the outside world.

Toby Strauss of Charcol Online says he employs 'about thirty-five people, I think', which pretty much sums it up – when you're growing at that kind of speed, it's difficult to work out even how many people currently work for you. From zero to thirty-five in just six months is a fairly slow speed of growth in the internet space, but it's extremely fast compared to any other sort of business. Strauss has gone out of his way to ensure that the business has grown at a manageable speed. The company has adjusted its marketing spend in order to speed up or slow down growth, consciously choking off consumer demand when it could be growing quicker, so that it can keep a lid on its own expansion. He is dismissive of companies, particularly web development agencies and other supplier organizations, that ratchet up their growth to the highest possible gear as early as possible. 'I don't see how companies like the web development shops can grow at the speed they do and keep any sense of a company culture,' he says. 'How can I feel part of something when there are ten new people arriving every week? Ultimately, it's more important that your existing staff are happy, and have a sense of being part of something and an understanding of what the aims of the business are.'

Even so, Charcol Online is growing at a pace which clearly leaves Strauss breathless. It's not just an issue of finding new people; more mundane infrastructural issues also weigh heavily, right down to the question of office space. The company is currently based in a kind of ante-chamber to its older cousin in a particularly unprepossessing bit of London's square mile. It's a prime if rather grim location for a company, and has considerably more cachet than the offices of most internet players. But as Strauss admits, that kind of prime location is not particularly suitable for a lot of the activities carried out there. For instance, the online business has its own in-house call centre, and that's currently housed in the expensive, inner-city offices, rather than the massive city-hinterland barns more usually associated with that industry. And the offices are by definition extremely limited in size. 'We're already running short of space,' says Strauss, cheerfully enough (it's only to be expected, after all). 'We're about to take over the top floor of the building we're in, and we'll probably have to move out of London next year. But, as we develop automated links with the lenders, that will reduce the need for us to have so many processing staff.'

As Strauss's words indicate, even more serious than the infrastructural issues that growth raises are the human issues it highlights. If you're growing at the rate he gives as an example (and I've certainly heard of growth rates of ten people a week more than once from companies and departments with staffing levels in the low three figures), you have to define the inter-relationships of people within the business as early as possible. For all the consultant-speak about flat manage-ment structures, hierarchies happen, and they're particularly necessary in a company where most of the employees are likely not to have been in their job long, and job definitions and the roles of specific individuals can be fluid. It's not like an organization where positions have already been defined, and new people can just slot into them; when most newcomers also have newly-created jobs, it's paramount that they know whom they are answerable to and what their specific role is, in so far as you can do that without stifling their flexibility and adaptability.

It's difficult to keep people motivated and happy in

the context of such growth. People will struggle to feel part of something cohesive if the size of the company is doubling every few months. On a basic level, they'll find it hard to keep track of who all the new people are. More fundamentally, they'll lose a sense of their own role and start caring more about where they stand within the organization than where it stands in the wider world. One of the great joys of working with the internet is that the rules are still being written, and that can breed great dedication to the business, a feeling of us-against-the-world. You can lose that if you expand too fast, and people's priority changes from being the direction of the business to their own direction within the business. People are always self-interested, but they need to see their own success and the success of the wider enterprise as inextricably bound together, otherwise they might just as well go off to another internet company for a few thousand pounds more – something they often do.

Keeping staff motivated and creating a dynamic company culture are not just problems of growth. They affect every business, whether new or old, growing or static, but particularly in the case of the internet world with its structure of early-stage businesses or business units. A lot of the time people are working long hours for something which might not work out; they are putting in a lot of effort on the basis that something might be very successful in the future. Internet-only businesses have the advantage of being able to create a corporate culture from scratch; every single action they take informs the culture of the company and the direction it will take. For an established business, it is not so clear-cut, but the internet does present an opportunity to breathe new life into stagnant workplaces, and to create a new sort of atmosphere and a new set of working conditions. Hence the decision of an increasing number of businesses to spin off their internet operations as a separate, semi-autonomous business. Tesco has created Tesco.com, and big financial services institutions like the Prudential, the Co-operative Bank and Abbey National have not only separated out their internet divisions, but also given them whole new brand identities: egg, smile and Cahoot respectively. Whatever you think about the advisability of these as brand names, they do give the companies several key advantages, not least of which is the opportunity to offer different prices from the parent company in an attempt to win new customers with what often amount to loss-leading offers. But equally important is the role they can have in staff motivation; as well as potentially being able to give staff equity in the new business at a stage when you almost certainly wouldn't have been able to give it to them in the traditional business, they have the effect of creating a new corporate identity for staff as well as for customers. Exciting, sexy new egg can recruit people that the fuddy-duddy old Pru never could; it is also likely to be able to keep them better, because it can shape culture and working conditions around the needs and desires of that new breed of employee, rather than attempting to slot people into an existing way of doing things that may not be appropriate for them.

As companies grow, integrating new staff becomes ever more difficult. They may not know their place in the organization, and the knock-on effect may be confusion among existing staff. It may also lead to resentment among existing staff. This has a lot to do with the different sorts of people a business recruits at different times in its growth.

When a company is in its early stages, it just needs to get clever people, and get them quickly. The chances of attracting someone who's smart and also has a bucketload of relevant experience are pretty slim, especially as remuneration is likely to be based around success in the future, rather than big bucks now. It has to take who it can get, and work with that raw material. As the company grows and becomes more successful, the calibre of the people it can attract becomes higher. So people may join with more skills, more experience, who are possibly more valuable to the business.

The dilemma is: do you ask those people to work for existing employees, who may well be less capable, or do you ask existing employees to work for these johnny-come-latelys? Everyone has to recognize that the people who join early are the ones taking the risk, staking their own future on the future success of the company, and that they deserve to be rewarded for that. But how that works operationally is a difficult one to resolve. In the high-tech industries of Silicon Valley in the US, where an entrepreneurial culture has surrounded the technology industry since long before the web became the mainstream business tool it is now, the answer has generally been a compromise. It has involved giving the long-serving, trusted employees special roles which don't fit into the standard chain of command, in order to avoid new and old staff rubbing up against each other and creating friction.

This is an issue which affects internet-only companies much more than established players. If the internet is an unproven part of what your company does, then persuading good people to come across from other parts of the business, or from outside it, might initially be tough. But as the internet operations expand and its role become bigger and more defined, attracting the best people should become easier, and at this point you'll find yourself facing these issues in exactly the same way that a dotcom would.

Similarly, it is hard for visionaries to know what their role is in an established business. New businesses, or new business areas for established companies, need visionary, dynamic people to get them off the ground. But when the emphasis shifts from making things happen at speed to growing sustainably and running a proper, grown-up business, those visionaries may no longer be the right people to be in charge. Tim Jackson, for example, was the brains behind online auction giant QXL. He came up with the idea, recruited the team to work for him, grew the company fast and took it as far as IPO. He then stepped back, became a non-executive director, took another job (for a venture capital company) and handed over the running of the business to Jim Rose, former chief executive of United Information Services, a division of United News and Media, chief executive of Blackwell Information Services, and managing director of Dun & Bradstreet/AC Nielsen. It was an acknowledgement on Jackson's part that his skill was in getting the company going, turning a great idea into a great company, rather than in the ongoing management of that company.

Ernesto Schmidt at Peoplesound.com admits that trying to take more of a back seat and let his business run itself has been a wrench. As the man who came up with the idea, wrote the business plan, raised the cash to kick it all off, recruited the initial team and built the whole thing from the ground up, it's been difficult to accept that other people have to run the day-to-day operations, and that his role is a strategic, long-term one.

'Having gone through the entire process of having the idea, working out the business plan, assembling the team and raising the money, you go through the opposite process to the one you usually go through in business,' he says. 'Usually you take a job and get more responsibility as time goes on and you become more senior. As boss of a dotcom, you actually have to have less and less involvement in the day-to-day running of it as it grows.'

Steve Bennett at jungle.com works hard to make sure his staff feel motivated and inspired. When Software Warehouse had a physical retailing arm, he would spend two days a month driving round to the stores and talking to the people who work there. Bennett doesn't believe that the transformation into jungle has made any real difference to the core values of the company. In fact, the company has those values enshrined on, of all things, a pack of playing cards. Bennett had previously put Software Warehouse's core values down on paper, and because they hadn't changed much, he just adapted them for jungle. The playing cards are certainly more memorable than the average corporate mission statement. The messages on them range from 'APPRECIATION – We do not take one another for granted and make a point of expressing our appreciation' to 'TAKING RISKS – We are willing to take calculated risks to stay competitive', taking in 'NEGATIVES – We openly discuss negative issues, but we never tolerate negative Team Members' en route.

To the jaded business eye, this all looks pretty

cheesy and, well, American, but it appears to be working. The company is clearly doing something right in terms of motivating and inspiring its staff: in 1999, its staff churn rate was just 2.85 per cent from a total of around 500 people. That may change as a result of the recent takeover of the company by GUS.

The internet exacerbates many of the human resources issues that all businesses face. The internet economy has grown, and continues to grow, at huge speed. That means that the supply of people can't keep up with the demand for people, particularly for people in more senior jobs. The only answer is to recruit from outside. The most common mistake is to look too hard for directly relevant experience of the internet, and to headhunt exclusively from direct competitors. Who's going to be more valuable to an internet travel business – someone with a year's experience of web development, or someone with twenty years' experience of the travel industry? Internet companies have become attractive places to work; it's a matter of selling a particular business to people. That doesn't mean simply splashing huge sums of money around, or handing out stock options or equity like sweets. It means building an attractive working environment where staff are encouraged, nurtured, and made to feel valued. If a company has deep enough pockets, getting staff is always possible, but in a market where good people can pick and choose their employer, and regular job moves are common (I know people who've worked for five different internet companies in two years), keeping staff is the real trick.

When businesses are growing at such speed,

management time tends to be focused on short-term fire-fighting; long-term planning can go out of the window, and staff development can easily slip to the bottom of the list. Working in an internet company can seem like an uphill struggle. People are going to be working long hours, and can easily become demotivated. The most important job of any manager is to make sure that doesn't happen; because in the internet space more than anywhere else, getting and keeping the best people can make or break a business.

CHAPTER FOUR

MONEY

The internet has prompted a lot of talk about goldrushes. It's the place where fortunes are supposed to be made, where 23-year-olds can become multi-millionaires within months, where companies can revive their flagging fortunes and send their revenues and share prices rocketing. Of course, it's also supposed to be the place where investors lose their sense of perspective, spending soars out of control, and no one ever makes a profit. The two are not unconnected.

Most dotcoms are in a high-risk business. The investment is large, the spend is large, the possible future riches are large, and the chances of failure are large. Established companies have more of a choice, and in many ways face less of a risk. The reason is obvious. An internet-only operator is staking its shirt on the success of what it does online. The future of an established business might also depend on how successfully it embraces these new media; but equally, it might not do.

Dotcoms tend to spend a lot of money, and try to attract similarly large amounts in funding, because of the fiercely competitive nature of the market they operate in. It's a small market which is growing at a massive speed, with a huge number of players, only a few of whom will ultimately be successful. In that context, grabbing as much market share as you can as quickly as possible is imperative. If you're starting from scratch, trying to build up a business from a standing start, spending heavily – on marketing, on technology, on people, on everything – looks like it could be a necessity.

This has become a kind of taken-as-read credo among internet companies. You need to raise a lot of money, and you need to spend a lot of money, otherwise you'll be nowhere. The common view is that if a company doesn't spend far in advance of its earnings, it will never be able to grow big enough quickly enough to be a serious player. Spending money faster than you can make it sounds like madness, and by any traditional way of judging the viability of a business, it is. But among new businesses that need to grab market share quickly, it's frequently seen as the only option they have. Peoplesound.com's Ernesto Schmidt, for example, says that he 'sneezes and spends half a million pounds'. And here's Brent Hoberman, co-founder of lastminute.com:

'If we'd had a small ambition – to be a small, moderately successful UK holiday site, say – then we wouldn't have achieved much. You have to work across a range of products and places, and you have to invest heavily. The definition of being visionary is investing before time.

'Launching lastminute.com wasn't just about us putting a flag in the ground and saying: "Here's a good idea – now somebody go and do it properly." We went harder and faster than anyone who wanted to follow us. It meant we got brand-name investors, it meant we got a credible board, and it meant we were able to invest in the right technology. If we hadn't done all that, and if we hadn't been so ambitious, we wouldn't have been able to dominate the market.'

The problem comes when this gets taken too far, and the culture of massive investment in order to grab market share starts to lead the business around by the nose. If a company wears its massive spending, well beyond its means, as a badge of honour, and feels it's not doing its job properly unless it's investing more than it can make, how is it ever going to make a profit? The answer, in most internet companies' case, is that profit is something distantly forecast for about four or five years' time. For a while, this was indulged by investors. This was the new-economy way of doing things, after all. If you expected a return on your investment quickly, you didn't understand the game. What you were investing in was the potential of these new businesses to dominate the medium of the future, not the reality of their revenues or profits or losses now. They had to lose money if they were going to win in the end. Internet stock values soared. Companies with revenues of a few million and little prospect of making a profit were suddenly capitalized at billions. Woe betide anyone who actually produced anything; that was old-economy business.

But you can't keep losing money for ever. In an increasing number of cases, highly-funded, high-spending internet companies started to find that things weren't as rosy as they thought. Boo.com went bust, and a number of seriously high-profile dotcoms in both the UK and the US such as music retailer

CDNOW, medical site Drkoop and natural health portal Clickmango started to experience cashflow difficulties. It only took a couple of well-publicized failures for previously sky-high investor confidence to take a shuddering dive. Companies that had previously had no problems whatsoever raising extravagant sums of cash, and had spent up to and beyond their means because they believed they could always go back and get more when they needed it, were suddenly finding that the VC bank had closed, and they weren't able to get the money they needed to sustain a company growing at such cash-draining speed.

In particular, the auditors of CDNOW, probably the best-known company in its category, announced that if it carried on spending at the same rate it could survive for only a few months longer. The company, which had been valued at more than a billion dollars, was eventually bought by media giant Bertelsmann for a paltry $117 million. Companies like CDNOW had been spending a lot, with no indication that they had the capacity to start making the sort of revenue that could push them towards profitability.

What had once seemed like the natural model for a new-economy business – spend more than you can afford in the short-term to build market share – was suddenly starting to look as precarious as it sounds. Internet-spawned businesses started to learn that they weren't the special case they'd thought they were. They have to play by the same rules as everyone else. Naturally enough, unless they start to make a profit within a few years, they won't survive. Their future is staked as much on the patience of their investors as the quality of their businesses. Suddenly the world looks a lot rosier for old-world businesses, with old-fashioned things like established customer bases, established products and services, established revenue streams, and even established profits.

It's worth taking a moment to look at how internet companies are currently being funded. At the time of writing, the typical path for most British dotcoms is as follows. They secure initial seed funding, usually from private backers, typically of between half a million and a million pounds. They use this to get themselves up and running, and then immediately start to go after their first major funding round, typically of between five and ten million pounds. That's followed with second and possibly third rounds where even larger sums are raised, followed by the first round of public financing, that great dotcom nirvana, the initial public offering.

There are several different types of investor they can turn to. The classic one is the professional venture capital fund. Then there are so-called angel investors: cash-rich private individuals, often arranged into networks, who professionally invest in start-up businesses. Increasingly, all kinds of professional services and other companies, from big accountancy firms to strategy consultancies to, in one curious British example, a classified advertising publisher (free ads paper *Loot*) are getting in on the act, investing in and helping out new businesses.

Some interesting new hybrid companies have started to spring up to cater for the burgeoning internet start-up market. Incubators, for instance, are companies that invest in new companies, usually through relationships they have with other professional investors like VCs, and also provide a framework for those businesses to work in. That could include everything from providing staff to temporarily plugging gaps in a company's management team, to providing offices, to providing a network of contacts and other businesses for the company to use – something most investors will offer in some form or other. Incubators have sprung up because so many dotcom management teams are young and inexperienced, and have big gaps in their expertise that they need help with. Increasingly, whatever type of investors companies use, they're looking for ones that are strategically relevant, investors with something to offer beyond just money.

With all of these different types of investor, the levels of investment are high. This way of doing things is something the British internet market has borrowed from the US, with its long-established culture of high-investment, high-risk, high-spend entrepreneurialism, which existed in the technology sector long before the era of the dotcom. It was transplanted on any serious scale to Europe, with London as its centre, as recently as 1999. Before that, the standard way for an internet business to grow was organically, or possibly with a small amount of private external investment, just like the vast majority of start-up businesses in the UK always have. The idea that the natural way to do things consists of repeated rounds of massive external private financing, followed by an IPO, is a very recent one.

These levels of funding are born of the belief, as mentioned above, that companies have to be prepared to spend heavily if they want to be successful in the fast-growing internet space. The upshot is that internet companies often have what seems to be a limitless capacity to spend vast sums of cash.

This often results in some very reckless spending, when it becomes an end in itself; companies know they need to spend to succeed, but the focus gets shifted from the succeeding to the spending. Heavily-backed businesses suddenly find themselves extremely cash-rich. They're sometimes run by people with little management experience, and that can lead to a lack of fiscal control. It can be a lack of understanding of what constitutes a worthwhile expense and what doesn't. It can be a lack of negotiating nous when it comes to corporate buying and selling. And it can even be because the people in charge don't care: they have all this money, so they're going to spend it. Investors can play a part in this: if they've invested several million in a business, they don't want it to be sitting in a bank account, they want it to be spent on building the business.

An interesting study came from e-business consultancy E-INSIGHT. It looked at 300 internet start-ups, some of them heavily backed by venture capital, others with little or no external funding. It found that marketing and technology spending among the VC-backed companies were predictably astronomical, marketing in particular, whose spend averaged 67 per cent of the company's sales. For non-VC-backed companies, the figure was 26 per cent. The result? The VC-backed companies were predicted to make an average operating loss of 76 per cent of their sales, compared to 30 per cent for their non-VC-backed counterparts. The study concluded that retailers with only an internet presence, and no grounding in traditional retail or mail order, will struggle over the next four or five years, because only then will the internet market become large enough to support a sizeable number of internet-only players. Again, that sounds like good news for old-economy companies.

You couldn't get a more classic example of an internet company losing control of its spending than boo.com. The company burned up the £130 million it got from investors in about a year before finally going into liquidation in early 2000. There were a number of reasons, and they highlight some of the areas where internet companies are forced to spend heavily, and where it can get out of control.

At the most basic level, boo spent so highly and eventually failed because it aimed so high. The company was a phenomenally ambitious project. For a start, it was trying to sell across eighteen countries, in seven different languages. That meant having offices in all those countries, with all the set-up costs entailed. It also meant creating a web site tailored to each market, with content authored separately for each country. (The UK and the US may share a language in theory, but you can't use the same web site for both of them.) And it meant creating a pricing system which would allow the company to offer the same price globally if it wanted to, but also a different price in each country if necessary, handle multiple currencies, and translate prices between them. And that's without even thinking about the different tax regimes in each country: where a transaction originates, where an item is despatched from, where it's received, and where tax is payable.

Technology costs of this kind can easily spiral out of control. Fast-moving internet businesses which are the first to do what they do – and boo was certainly the first to try and set up in so many countries simultaneously – will usually have to build a lot of their own technology from scratch. That means employing top techies, and they don't come cheap. It's easier and cheaper for companies that aren't the first mover, because they can usually buy at least some of their technology off the shelf.

Boo was forced to face these issues head on. The multiple language problem was just one of them. There was also the problem of fashion industry databases; they tend to be short on fields which describe clothing items, because fashion industry buying is done in the flesh. There's no need for a lengthy description of an item if you can pick it up, but if price, size, colour and style are the only information you have about a product it's very difficult to categorize it in a database, or describe it meaningfully to a consumer. The result was that boo had to offer its users rotate and zoom pictures of all the items it sold – and getting enough pictures for that cost far more than the company anticipated. Then there's logistics, the need to build an order processing and fulfilment system that works across multiple countries; in boo's case, it had to work with partners that used different technology. And associated with that are all the non-technical costs like warehouses and delivery.

It highlights the problems of first-mover advantage. Boo had to create its technology from scratch rather than buy a ready-made product. And ironically, boo's technology was bought by software company Bright Station from its liquidator KPMG with exactly this purpose in mind: to sell it on as a technology platform for other e-tailers. Further, Boo employed hundreds and hundreds of people, most of them paid extremely generously. The company had gone down the route of paying high to attract the best people. That was a gamble which didn't pay off. Then there were expenses, with tales abounding of boo staff, however lowly, jetting off around the world first class and enjoying lavish entertainment at the company's expense. Other factors were the cost of the many offices, including its lavish HQ in London's Carnaby Street; the non-core activities, like the site's online lifestyle magazine *boom*, created in-house by a team of journalists, which started entirely divorced from the rest of the site, and was hastily integrated into the sales operation when it was found to be a big cash drain that didn't actually do anything for the bottom line; the cost of creating the actual boo.com web site, a visually-rich, animation-heavy eye-candyfest, created at huge expense by the company's web agency Organic; and finally, the marketing, a multi-million-pound campaign which managed the unique feat of breaking on national TV months before the site was even finished and ready to launch. More than anything else, it was this five-month launch delay that crippled the company. The cash continued to gush out, for all the reasons above, and there were no revenues to staunch the flow. When it finally did launch, income never approached being big enough to turn it around.

For dotcoms, the business of attracting funding and working out how best to spend it is a minefield. Established businesses can easily fall into the same trap, but in general, they have a slightly different set of problems. They can usually fund their internet development from existing revenues, so they don't have to take the same risks. They can cross-invest from their existing operations, they already have an established cashflow, and they know how to make profits. If they fail online, they can write off the money, pull out, reassess the situation and carry on. They won't have driven themselves into the ground like a dotcom would. It might be the death of them in the end, but it's not going to cause a short-term collapse, and they can always retrench and try again.

But there's a flipside to this. Whereas well-funded dotcoms are able to move at the incredible speed expected on the internet, traditional businesses are much less likely to be able to do so. Unless there's genuine faith from the very top of a company that the internet represents its future, any expenditure is likely to be experimental. It might be at a level low enough that the company will make only a small loss, or even a modest profit, out of its internet operations, but there's a danger that if the investment isn't there, those operations won't amount to much. Rivals will spend higher, and move faster. It's the classic dilemma for an old-economy business.

An increasingly popular option is to spin off a company's internet operations as a separate business, or at least as a totally independent unit. That way, it becomes self-financing, operates more like a dotcom, and can even in some cases look at alternative funding sources from outside the company. As mentioned in Chapter 3, spin-off companies can often reward their staff, for instance in the form of stock options or equity, in a way that their parent companies can't. It's also a good way of realizing the value of a company's internet business, which may make up quite a small percentage of its revenues, but which, if assessed independently, may turn out to be worth as much to investors as the rest of the company put together. Dixons made the decision very early in the life of Freeserve that it should spin its internet business off as a separate company and float it. The result was that Freeserve was quickly worth more than its parent. Spin-offs also spread risk away from the parent company; no one knows what will work in the long term, but if they're going to take the internet seriously and invest heavily in it, businesses may consider it worth distancing themselves from their high-risk online ventures.

With cash moving through internet companies at frightening speeds, they're particularly prone to the cashflow problems that afflict all high-growth businesses, particularly start-ups. For that reason, payment in equity has become an increasingly popular option. Instead of paying fees, more and more internet companies are offering a chunk of their equity to services companies, whether they be in web design, law, accountancy or even PR. It is a way of guaranteeing commitment and quality of service from a supplier, because they suddenly have a very compelling reason for wanting the business to succeed as well. It can also signal a shortage of cash. If a company believes in what it's doing, and thinks it's going to make a lot of cash out of it, then its own stock is the most valuable thing it possesses. It's questionable why it would want to give some of that value away, when a cash payment would suffice; it can imply that the company has no cash.

Procter & Gamble has been involved in some fairly startling examples of seeking alternative funding from outside the main company. It's really not something you would ever imagine an organization like P&G doing. But the launch in 1999 of its personalized online beauty service reflect.com heralded a new era for the company. P&G's former European internet chief Frederic Colas explains reflect.com thus: 'Reflect is not about a product, or a service, or even several products or services. It's an experience brand. That experience has one key attribute, which is personalization. The outcomes of that personalization are products or services. What reflect is selling is an experience. The brand is defined by a total solution which is personal to you. It shows there's a future in personalization of products where the price is low. They're finding out if they can do mass customization. It's a learning process.'

Reflect.com is structured as a separate company from P&G, but it's part-owned by the packaged goods giant. The founders of reflect came from within P&G, but instead of running it as part of the parent company, they went away and set it up as a separate organization.

'P&G should be able to do reflect and the like internally,' says Colas. 'But it will be some time before it can. There are major cultural issues. Think about how P&G looks at one dollar of investment. P&G invests one dollar to have a chance to make a little more than 15 per cent return on investment annually. The company takes a small risk to maximize the chance of making a profit that is good, but it's not the jackpot. That's the P&G-side way of looking at it. But from the venture capitalists' side, they'll invest one dollar knowing that they have an 85 per cent chance of losing it, but maybe a ten per cent chance of making twenty dollars. So when it comes to investing in a very risky digital venture, it's time to get that dollar from a VC, rather than from P&G.'

In this case, P&G and reflect have taken the view the internet moves at such a speed that it demands risk-taking, VC-style investment to really succeed, rather than the fiscally cautious approach that characterizes most established organizations. As Colas points out, there's a difference in investor expectations which affects the ability old-world businesses have to compete with new players. The expectation of anyone who invests in a dotcom is that a lot of money will be spent very quickly, and the company won't move into profitability for a while. But for people who own any other type of company, whether they be private owners or the shareholders of a publicly traded company, internet expenditure is only a part of a far bigger whole. When its value is being assessed, it is being assessed alongside a lot of other types of expenditure. And whereas some of them will have an obvious, immediate value on the bottom line, it is rare that an internet project will do the same. Persuading the people who control the purse-strings that big investment is required with uncertain short-term returns isn't easy. They will quite justifiably baulk at the massive quantities of cash being poured into something which brings no immediate discernable benefit, especially as it will almost certainly take cash away from other parts of the business. A solid business case has to be made for high-spend, high-risk investment within organizations with little history of such spending. It has to be sold as an essential investment for the future, not a mindless cash drain.

It may mean that traditional companies will suffer

from their inability to move quickly enough in this hyper-growth, constantly-changing economy. But speed isn't always a good thing. Companies have to move fast for the right reasons: because they recognize the dizzying speed of change and how they can profit from it, rather than because they find themselves in a blind panic and desperately feel the need to do something, anything, quickly. One of the greatest dangers for any company using the internet is that it can find itself moving faster than the business can cope with. If a company moves much faster than it ever has before, it risks launching operations that don't do justice to its core business, and which compromise its brand. It also risks organizational chaos.

Established businesses that do decide to invest heavily in the internet can still face some of the same problems as their dotcom rivals. The internet can still be a bottomless pit when it comes to investment. Marketing, technology, human resources, physical infrastructure, customer service – the costs mount fast. And it isn't always easy to know which to prioritize.

'One of the most difficult things is that the number of things you can to improve is almost limitless – to improve customer service, the experience, whatever,' says Marks & Spencer's head of e-commerce Peter Robinson. 'The problem is knowing what you can achieve in the timescale you have available, and what you can afford. Prioritizing what to do is very difficult, because you're comparing the relative importance of a lot of very different things.'

However an internet company spends its money, the bottom line is that it has to be able to judge how successful that investment has been. That means understanding what the real business objectives of an organization's internet activities are, and setting targets that will be used to judge success. It may mean focusing on return on investment, but it will certainly mean identifying and setting at the very start a reliable way to judge the organization's success online. It has to be judged on its own merits, even if the expenditure is regarded within the company as experimental. There have to be set objectives.

That has always been the case with Charcol Online, which has been able to attract continued investment from its parent company precisely because targets were set, and then met. 'When I joined John Charcol, the money was just injected that was required to get it going,' says Charcol Online's managing director Toby Strauss. 'We've been ahead of plan ever since, so there hasn't been a problem with the funding. The company's owners made it clear that £20-£30 million would be made available. We had no problem getting the first £10 million, and hopefully, because we're ahead of plan, we won't have any problem getting hold of the rest.'

There is a lot of money sloshing around the internet. That doesn't mean that everyone with a half-baked idea for a dotcom gets funded, and it doesn't mean it's easy for existing companies to justify the sort of expenditure they need to create a compelling web presence. It still requires a company's top-level management to buy into the idea of the internet. The level of investment required can all too easily look like a cash drain with no demonstrable benefit to the company.

Financial conservatism isn't necessarily a bad thing where the internet is concerned. It isn't quite as much of a goldrush as you might think. For most companies, it's about working out the right level of investment, justifying why that sort of money is needed, and then spending it prudently. Businesses need to treat money exactly as they always did. They need to be hard-headed about investment; control their spending, while acknowledging that they may need to invest at speeds that wouldn't usually be justified; look closely at risk, assess their attitude to it, and take decisions accordingly; and set targets and be focused on the bottom line.

The aim of every business is still to be profitable. Amid all the sound and fury, it's easy to lose sight of that. The majority of profitable internet-only businesses are still web sites selling pornography. Established businesses, as much as dotcoms, need to be able to demonstrate a path to profitability, how all this investment will eventually benefit the company. If they can do that, they have a much better chance of working out how much they should be investing.

CHAPTER FIVE

MARKETING

Marketing has, so far, been the heart and soul of the internet economy. Unfortunately, in most cases, it has spectacularly failed to be the brain.

If you're a new company operating in the internet space, or a traditional company which has changed around what it does because of the internet, you need to let potential customers know about you. Marketing is the way you do this. The problem is that you're likely to be doing it from a standing start, when they may not have ever heard of you before. You need to get across to your target customer group who you are, what you do, and why they should use you. And you have to do so very quickly, because the economy you're operating in is growing at the speed of light, and if you don't tell everyone who you are very quickly, a competitor will jump in, you will have lost what is generally referred to as first-mover advantage and you'll be left behind. How to counteract this? Well, obviously, you need to spend a lot of money marketing yourself in the most aggressive way possible, as quickly as you can.

So much for the theory. The practice is rather different, because there are quite a few problems with building a business this way.

The common mistake most companies operating in the internet space make – and this applies particularly to the dotcoms – is to assume that a load of advertising equals a brand. Companies desperate for first-mover advantage are trying to jump-start their brand building and get critical mass quickly. In these times of indiscriminate mass-market ads for internet companies, it's easy to start thinking that a big marketing spend equals a big brand. It doesn't. Companies that spend their money unwisely will get nothing. Even ones that spend it well won't automatically get a great brand, because marketing can't make a brand on its own; high name recognition is not the same as a good brand.

If you scatter enough ads out there, the reasoning goes, then you have a brand. You don't, what you have is a name that people recognize. But that on its own will never be enough to make people engage with you, visit your web site, buy from you, or do whatever you want them to do with you online. You cannot make your product or service meaningful to consumers simply by shouting your name repeatedly from the rooftops – it just becomes a word that they hear a lot. US online music retailer CDNOW has fantastic name recognition, particularly in its home market, where it's about the best-known online music retailer there is. But that didn't stop it running into massive financial difficulties and getting bought out cheaply.

Excessive haste is the main culprit. If you're desperate to get an ad campaign within the next two weeks, you're probably not going to get a good one. Partly that's because the creative work and the media buying will be rushed, and partly because companies trying to move at that speed rarely take the time before they embark on their marketing drive to work out what it is that their brand actually stands for. And even if you do successfully work out the brand values you want to project, you can't just say them lots of times and expect people to believe them. People's perception of your brand is shaped by their experience of it. It is a collection of values built around the benefits people believe they'll get if they use a particular product or service. It is what makes people spend more than they need to when they buy something. A brand is about emotion, and that emotion comes from experience; you can't build it in a vacuum with a load of billboards.

So when someone enters a particular retailer, or a particular hotel, or picks up a certain item of clothing, or a cosmetic product, everything about it is helping to shape that brand for that person: atmosphere, service, packaging and so on. You can't just *tell* people you stand for certain things – you actually have to stand for them. So many people's experience of using commercially-driven services on the internet is one of a functional, personality-free, clunky environment, where customer service is scary and impersonal, fulfilment is unreliable and the overriding feeling is of isolation and alienation. You can't get away with this. If you're going to trumpet certain brand values, you have to live up to them.

Here, again, boo.com is a good example. The company tried to create a brand with the colour and emotion of offline retail brands, as far away as possible from the bland, price-driven, unexciting nature of most online shopping experiences. Unfortunately, in its desperation to be cool, the site forgot to be functional. The front-end interface was treated as a visual design issue, and the result was a site that looked pretty, but was very hard to use on all but the most advanced computers. So the site didn't deliver on its promise to be an exciting, fun shopping environment. The advertising created excitement around the brand, which was first frustrated by the site's lengthy launch delay, and then let down by the experience of using it.

Marketing can be a very valuable part of building a brand by reinforcing and helping to shape the emotional associations a product or service has for people, but it's only a part. And advertising is just a subset of marketing, one of the many ways a company can spend its marketing budget. That hasn't stopped internet companies relying on advertising in a knee-jerk way as the thing they have to do in order to build a brand and get market share. Often it doesn't have the effect of building a brand at all.

Advertising can also be used to drive response. It helps if the brand is already familiar to its target audience. Too many internet companies advertise as if their audience ought to be familiar with the brand. They are having brand values attributed to them that they simply don't have in most people's minds – they only have them in the bubble of their own advertising. They won't acquire those values unless the companies themselves can live up to the promises implicit in their advertising, something they often fail to do. And they won't drive response until those values are something the target audience recognizes and feels an affinity with, rather than abstractions, dreamed up in isolation, with little or no connection to the product.

Internet companies start to make difficulties for themselves when they walk into advertising agencies and say something along the lines of: 'Hello, we want some ads.' That in itself may not be a problem, but it will be if they add: 'And we need them finished by next month.' It means that they probably haven't properly worked out what they stand for before they get to the stage of getting the ads made. Good marketing comes from a good brand: you have to know what you stand for before you can tell people all about it. This sounds pretty obvious, but that hasn't stopped a spate of ads for internet-related services with a core proposition something along the lines of 'We're a web site where you can go and do things.'

If an advertising agency is any good, it will think about the brand of an internet product or service in exactly the same way it would think about pretty much any other brand, and create ads based on that brand's values accordingly. The alarm bells should start ringing if an agency has a couple of vaguely techno-literate creatives, and chucks all the internet accounts in their direction. The problem with pigeonholing what you do in an internet ad is that you're more than likely to get globes with arrows going round them and suchlike – generic internet-communications-technology-isn't-it-great type stuff. You'll end up with an ad about the internet, not an ad about what that company can do for its customers.

Trying to move too fast is always dangerous. Haste is a wonderful killer of creativity, and of clear, sensible thinking. Even if you have taken the time out to think out properly what your brand does, it can be tempting to bang an ad out in a week so that you get that crucial first-mover advantage. But it's a sure recipe for bad ads.

The internet is a medium where companies ought

to be able to identify their customer group, find those people and address them individually. One of the great ironies is that when it comes to attracting customers, most internet companies reach straight for the complete opposite: the least targeted, most scattergun marketing approach there is, mass-market advertising. TV, the national press, billboards, taxis, buses and the London Underground – they've all become plastered with well-funded, big-spending dotcoms, desperate to get their names out to as many people as possible. This sort of mass-market, scatter-gun approach that characterizes the way internet companies have been advertised so far simply isn't appropriate for most organizations. Most companies' marketing will have more to do with identifying a customer group and then targeting it in relevant places with relevant messages. According to Steve Bennett, even jungle.com, which is one of the biggest mass-market spenders, has found that the humble, cheap, old-fashioned trade press is still the most cost-effective of all the advertising media it uses to reach its customers. Most companies are either too small, too niche- or business-focused to worry about mass-market consumer promotion. Especially if they're smaller players, they'll have to extract maximum value from their marketing, and so they need to approach it in a more scientific fashion. The crucial thing is to address the relevant audience in the relevant way. It's a lesson that some of the big-spending mass-market brands would do well to heed.

It's as basic as this: businesses need to work out who their customers are and target them accordingly. If they're the same people they target in the physical world, they don't need to do anything very different from before. Their brand values won't have changed that much, and so if they advertise, the creative executions and choice of media are going to be similar. The real challenge will be to make sure that the online experience they give people fits with the brand values they're looking to promote. They might also find that they need to advertise more than they used to, to give their internet services a push, but they need to avoid assuming that they need to do something completely different from what they've always done in order to attract those people.

If they're trying to widen or change their customer base, it all becomes a bit more complex. It's something that John Charcol faced when it launched Charcol Online. As mentioned earlier, the company has had to become a lot more mass-market in the way it promotes itself, because it now offers its service for free, opening it up to a much broader range of potential customers.

The company is suddenly having to explain a complex proposition to a very broad range of people. So it has had to go from being a company that has never tried to promote itself in a major way, to one which is forced to advertise. The company has gradually upped its advertising spend, cautiously at first, but latterly with increasing confidence. The change has also affected the type of advertising the company has run, and the media the company has used. Suddenly, it has a whole new group of potential customers who don't understand what it does. It needs to get across the fact that people can choose between a huge range of products, some of them exclusive to the service, without having to pay for the privilege. Its ads have focused very much on the idea that the lenders are effectively competing for an individual borrower's business, something which appears to put them in charge – a reversal of the usual roles. So as well as appearing in the personal finance media that John Charcol has traditionally used, the ads have also appeared on personal finance web sites, and in more mainstream media such as national newspapers.

'We're thinking about how much our advertising spend should be long-term, in terms of how fast we want to grow,' says Charcol Online managing director Toby Strauss. 'There's a natural speed of growth for a company, and you implode if you grow too fast. The thing that has the biggest impact on your growth is your spend on marketing – that's the knob that we turn.'

The company ran its first big campaign on the sides of London taxis in June 1999. In the spring of 2000 it ran a campaign on the London Underground. But what Strauss describes as the bedrock of the campaign is in the press, both the specialist personal finance press and the national newspapers.

'We're looking at TV, but TV isn't really a response-based medium, and it's not clear to us that we really need to build our brand. Many of our competitors are spending a lot of money on advertising, and they're spending that money partly to build the mortgage brokering market in the UK. I'd rather that my competitors are spending to build the whole market, rather than me spending to build it, which will partly benefit them as well.'

It's a point well made, and another argument against generic advertising with a lack of real brand differentiation. If a company just says, 'You can do X on the web, and you can use our site to do it', then it's probably going to be expanding the market for its online competitors as much as for itself. If it doesn't give people specific reasons to use its service rather than that of a competitor, it shouldn't be surprised if it finds that its marketing spend is helping other companies as much as it is helping the company itself.

The message here is that for all the high-spend media opportunities that cash-rich internet companies are finding open to them, the traditional methods can still be the most effective. And they're not necessarily the methods that cost the most, either.

Like Strauss, Chris Hall of Dell has found that the lower-cost print media his company has traditionally always used as its main way of promoting itself are still the most effective. 'Our main method of original lead generation is still the trade press,' he says. 'We also have things like affiliate programmes, which are an extremely low-cost and cost-effective way of doing business, but the amount of business they generate is a very small proportion of the whole.'

Companies can get people to come to a web site in any number of different ways, but ultimately, if their aim is to sell to them, the number of people who come to the site is irrelevant – it's the number who buy that matters. So while a poster and TV blitz might catch the eyes, it might not get the people who are seriously interested in buying in the same way that, say, a targeted ad in the computer press would for Dell. 'The conversion rate – comparing the number of people who come onto our site with the number who buy – is very small,' says Hall. 'Half of our traffic never even goes into the store part of the site. We need to maximize the number who buy, not just the number who come.'

Jungle.com is one company which has spent big; its huge spending was a big factor in its recent buyout. The company took the view that it needed to spend a lot in order to establish market share for itself. It launched with a first-year marketing budget of £7.5m, which it is set to exceed, with £750,000 spent before it had even launched. According to figures from research company AC Nielsen MMS, that made it the eighth biggest offline ad spender to promote internet services in the UK in the second half of 1999 and the first half of 2000. The strategy was born of the company's desire to get its name out there and establish itself as a well-recognized British retailer. The company was reasonably well known in its previous incarnation, as mail order and store-based retailer Software Warehouse; the decision to launch its internet business under a different name meant that it had to build consumer confidence, retailing credibility and all those other things that make a strong retail brand all over again. There was also an issue of timing; unlike, say, eBay, jungle launched in August 1999 – pretty late in the day to try and establish an e-tail brand from scratch. According to managing director Steve Bennett, the nature of the core products it sells – computer-related items of relatively high value – was also a factor.

'We did a massive advertising campaign at the time of our launch, because you need to work very hard to gain enough consumer confidence so that people will buy something with a much higher order value than a book or CD over the internet,' he comments.

The result was a massive ad blitz, timed to coincide with the company's launch. It took in press, posters, public transport, radio and, eventually, TV – in other words, most of the mass-media advertising opportunities around. In fact, the ads were so widespread and so effective that they resulted in the site being deluged with customers.

As befits a man who's clearly nonplussed by other sites' lack of research into the effectiveness of their marketing, Bennett can clearly see which types of ad are the most effective, which he should be stepping up and which he should be ditching. And he's found, unsurprisingly enough, that ads targeted at computer enthusiasts – in his case, in computer magazines – have been the most effective and the best value for money. 'Vertically targeted advertising is always most effective,' he says. He also rates newspapers highly for their broad appeal, TV for its penetration and taxis because they get him a lot of exposure for relatively little money. The company's most cost-effective form of marketing, though, is its e-mail list. Jungle.com encourages visitors to its site to sign up to receive regular e-mails from it. They can specify which subjects they want to be e-mailed about, and how often they want to receive them. The cost of marketing to these people, says Bennett, is close to zero, and the response he gets from doing so is higher than from almost any other type of marketing the company does.

Jungle.com is unusual in having done a lot of both the development of its brand and that brand's values, and the creative work that followed, in-house. During the initial stages, it didn't use any agencies. Bennett himself came up with the name, and an in-house team developed the original creative concepts. The initial technical development of the site was also undertaken in-house.

The company later appointed advertising agencies to help it take its message to the public, but swiftly changed agencies because it didn't feel the advertising was hard-nosed enough. Once again, Bennett's focus on the principles of direct marketing, and being able to drive sales very directly from ads, came to the fore when the decision was made. 'Our original agencies were fantastic at brand advertising, but they don't really understand retail advertising. They're not good at response-driven ads. It needs to be really hard, in-your-face stuff.'

Bennett believes that the in-house route has served his company very well, but he doesn't recommend it for everyone. In particular, he's scathing about a lot of attempts by internet companies to do their own media buying. It may be cheaper, but, he reasons, if you've no experience of doing it, you'll probably do it very badly indeed. 'You can waste marketing money so easily if you haven't done it before. There's some staggeringly naive media buying going on. I've talked to people in internet companies who don't even negotiate on rate. I asked someone what the ratecard was for some posters he'd bought, and he told me, and then I asked him what he'd actually paid, and it was the same amount. He didn't even understand the difference between ratecard and the price you actually pay. People are wasting so much money like that.'

If there's naive media buying like this going on, then it's only natural that media owners will take advantage of it by charging as much as they can get away with. There's an issue of sheer supply and demand here. With all the new internet players rushing to market, desperate to establish their brands in the public mind, seeing mass-market advertising as the best way to do so and willing to pay large amounts of cash to ensure their message gets out there, prices are bound to rise. The increase in demand for advertising space outstrips the increase in media outlets, particularly ones that reach enough relevant people to be worth bothering with. Ratecards rise and, insidiously, media owners have started to operate differential pricing policies – if you're an internet company, you automatically get charged more. It can't continue in the long term, but the surge in demand for ad space means that it's allowed to happen. Advertisers are desperate to get their message out and media owners know that. It means that advertisers don't really have a choice.

It means too that a lot of internet companies with big marketing budgets are throwing their money away. Dotcoms, in particular, don't have an established brand they can take online, and so they have to explain what their brand stands for from first principles, as well as what their web site allows people to do. They feel pretty much forced to spend more on advertising. Add in the deep pockets and the need to get to market quickly which the heavily venture capital-backed companies have, and you have a recipe for hyper-inflated ad spend, and the sort of blanket dotcom advertising that we've seen over the last year.

Research company AC Nielsen MMS's figures on how much companies are spending on traditional media advertising to promote internet services bear this out. In an average month, eleven of the twenty companies spending the most on offline advertising for internet services in the UK are pure-play dotcoms. On average, only four are established offline companies (BT and various financial services companies, mainly), with the rest made up of dotcom spin-offs from traditional players, like Freeserve and egg. Total spend to promote internet services between June 1999 and May 2000 was around £56m. A lot of money is flowing direct from venture capitalists to media owners. How much it achieves for the dotcoms whose hands it fleetingly passes through in the middle is questionable. Dotcoms are afflicted by a panicky need to shout their names as quickly and as often as possible in order to ensure that someone has at least heard of them. It's not healthy.

Marketing budgets are only the most visible example of a malady which afflicts internet companies across the board: spending for the sake of it. It's particularly visible with the dotcoms, whose cash usually comes from venture capitalists or other big-spending investors. But it's also true of established businesses moving online, particularly now they tend to be better funded. The money arrives in a big block – companies' internet operations often go from having very little money to suddenly having a lot – and they're constantly told that they're nowhere unless they build market share quickly. The way to do that, of course, is to spend money. It's a mentality which says: 'We've got money, so we're sure as hell going to spend it,' which leads to a lack of cost control. Rather than working out the most cost-effective way of running an advertising campaign, it can be easier to run into an ad agency with a big brick of cash and say: 'I want a fantastic ad, and I don't care how much it costs – just give me the best you've got.'

This is not, as you can probably imagine, an approach to be advised. The late boo.com, the UK's most famous internet failure, was famous for its huge

THE NET EFFECT

marketing budget. The company plastered its ads everywhere pretty indiscriminately, at a very early stage of its existence, so early that the site wasn't even working. You can imagine the result. Thousands of people visited the site, and were confronted with a message that the site hadn't launched yet but, er, they could leave their details if they wanted to. The level of expectation was huge, but the reality was disappointing. Brands are supposed to exceed people's expectations of them; boo did the opposite. It was a lack of joined-up thinking by the company; the ad campaign was booked to run at the time the site was due to launch; it then didn't launch on time, for a variety of technical and infrastructural reasons. The ads went out, and the result was chaos. It was a huge waste of money, and created consumer expectations which the site was completely unable to meet. Spending too much on marketing, and spending a lot of it unwisely, was a major contributory factor in boo's so-called burn rate, the rate at which a company uses up money faster than it makes it. The company knew it had to make a big noise to get the kind of audience its ambitious plan for world domination demanded, but it didn't keep any control on the way that money was spent; nor did it plan the campaign to have maximum impact for the money spent.

Indiscriminate marketing spends are particularly likely to happen when people running a company don't really understand marketing. And marketing is a favourite area for excessive spending because it's more or less a bottomless pit. It's not difficult to rack up an enormous bill for the creative work, and as for paying for the media, the sky's the limit, because more ads always looks better than less ads if you're trying to get customers in double-quick time. And it's always possible to book more ads.

Spending a lot doesn't necessarily build a brand. It can build a well-recognized name, but it won't even necessarily do that. A company with just about as high name recognition as you could hope for like lastminute.com doesn't feature in any of the top twenties of offline ad spenders among internet-related companies. Lastminute.com's Brent Hoberman is clear that while the company does need to spend money to build itself up and get critical mass, spending too much is as inadvisable as spending too little. 'We're at an early stage in our business. We have to invest in the brand, and in our human capital,' he says. 'But we've managed to get a lot of recognition by having such a good spokesperson.' By this he means his business partner and the company's co-founder, the much-photographed, much-interviewed Martha Lane Fox. 'People like success stories, and particularly British success stories. And we're in a sector that's the focus at the moment. E-commerce has been the sexy subject, and everyone wants to make sense of how to do it.'

True enough, but enthusiasm for a subject doesn't necessarily imply a totally benign attitude towards all of its practitioners. An over-reliance on PR as a marketing tool can be dangerously unstable – of which more later.

One of the biggest, most successful internet companies globally, eBay, hardly spent a cent on advertising in its first two years of existence. Instead, the company adopted a conscious policy of building its customer base from grass roots, rather than attempting to establish itself by shouting its name from the rooftops at a very early stage, before anyone knew what it was about.

The company is the world's largest online auction provider. It specializes in person-to-person auctions; someone puts an item up for sale, and anyone else can bid to buy it. It's a bit like a hyper-efficient, global, classified advertising service, the difference being that people can actually buy the items offered through the site, rather than having to contact the vendor directly. eBay likes to see itself as nothing more than an efficient global market-place for the trading of more or less anything.

That makes it a very attractive proposition among certain key customer groups. While pretty much anyone might be interested in selling via eBay, it's not difficult to identify who the enthusiasts are going to be. And so the company set out from the start to target these people: collectors, hobbyists, and anyone else with a passion for a particular activity or pastime. It targets them by going to collectors' fairs, forging links with hobbyists' groups, getting out there and meeting key people in those worlds face-to-face. Once it had talked to them and convinced them that it was a great place for them to buy and sell, the word was spread by personal recommendation among those communities of interest, which tend to be close-knit. What advertising the company did was limited to extremely small, low-volume, low-price media that targeted precisely those influential and potentially lucrative groups: if you're a keen gig-goer, you might have seen eBay ads on fliers, promoting it as the best place to buy and sell music and associated items; if you read football fanzines, you might find similar small ads aimed at people who collect footballing memorabilia. The advantages are clear: you reach a targeted group of people for a fraction of the price of a mass-media campaign, and your brand means something to them, because they experience it, rather than just seeing it as a name on an irritatingly wacky TV ad featuring a B-list celebrity and a collection of bad jokes.

The company's founder Pierre Omidyar is on record as saying that he doesn't believe that advertising is the most effective way to build a solid user-base. He prefers, where possible, to use word of mouth and ground-level promotion to build loyalty to and trust in his company's brand. In a perverse kind of way, he had it easy. At the time when the company was set up, in September 1995, eBay didn't have any competitors. It also didn't have much money, which meant that it didn't have too much choice when it came to promoting itself. That forced it to think smarter about how it targeted potential customers; in a perverse way, it was lucky not to have the option of using a lot of dumb money on big billboards. The undoubted advantage eBay had was time. Back when the company launched, the market was not packed with competitors. With a relatively clear market, eBay had time to build organically; it wasn't forced into aspiring to the kind of hyper-growth that results in ill-considered overspending on advertising. And even now, it still dominates the online auction market.

A company like M&S is in an unusual position when it comes to promoting what it does online. The company is more or less unique among major British corporates in so far as until recently it hadn't advertised. It hadn't needed to. The M&S brand is so strong, and the company has such a dominant market position, notwithstanding its recent problems, that ads would have been largely redundant. Now, however, M&S is advertising for the first time as its all-powerful position in British retailing has slipped. Allied to this, it's doing new things that it needs to tell people about – things like its online retailing operation. The company doesn't intend to rush headlong into big-spending, mass-market promotion of its new e-commerce service. Being M&S, it wants to get the service perfect before it promotes it. It has to; customers will not tolerate any imperfections, and M&S can't risk the damage a poor customer experience might do to its brand.

'It's about striking a balance between when to advertise and how to advertise,' says the company's head of e-commerce Peter Robinson. 'In terms of when, we do feel that we need to get to the point of being in a market-leading position before we shout about what we do. We don't want to let people down.'

The idea of getting to a market-leading position before starting to advertise is a startling reversal of the usual thinking among internet companies. The general rule is that massive sums of cash are spent on marketing campaigns precisely because companies want to get market share – that advertising is the way to achieve a market-leading position, not something you do when you get there.

As Robinson points out, this has a lot to do with the relative strength of various brands. 'Dotcoms have to shout about what they do,' he says, 'because no one knows who they are. We probably take more revenue than a lot of them do already, but we don't have to shout because everyone knows who we are.'

The company is planning to start doing some

serious shouting in late 2000, round about the time that this book publishes. Much of this will fall into the category of corporate advertising for M&S as a whole, which will include references to the company's e-commerce offering, and will use the web address as one of its main calls to action. 'It's not going to be indiscriminate, and it's not going to be from the rooftops,' says Robinson. 'It'll probably be from the second or third floor.'

One of the first branding issues companies need to face is what name to use on the internet. Do they take their existing name, and hopefully their existing brand, and transfer it online, form a new one for the internet, or form one which is linked to the main brand but has some independence from it. The issue is one of integration: how far a company wants to turn its internet operations into something separate from its main business, which stands on its own as an individual entity, and how far it wants to keep them integrated. Of course, setting up a new brand, or even a separate company, is more expensive and time-consuming than extending existing operations onto the internet. It's a more ambitious way of tackling the market. That doesn't mean it's right for everyone. But there are some advantages.

A new brand allows a company to create a new product offering or, just as importantly, a new pricing structure. The online element of an existing business will find itself in all sorts of trouble if it tries to sell cheaper than the offline element, unless it is made very clear that it's being done as an incentive. EasyJet, for example, gives its customers money off for booking on its web site. The message is clear: buying online is better for you, the customer. The company reckons that the amount it saves on processing each transaction it would otherwise have made by phone can compensate for the reduced price. It couldn't do this if it didn't have that explicit justification – if it tried to do it without telling people. If, say, M&S tried to offer clothing cheaper online than in the shops, its customers would revolt. M&S wants to keep its stores, and use the internet as an extra new channel rather than replace its existing ones, so it can't go down the online discounting route. But the likes of egg can offer better rates online than the Prudential offers in the physical world without harming the Prudential brand or making too much of an impact on its sales – any impact egg makes will be spread across the whole sector of competing companies. If egg had been the Prudential Online and offered better rates than the company does offline, it would have had a much more direct impact on its traditional operations, and would probably have raised a PR storm.

There's an issue of brand heritage to be addressed. Companies have to ask themselves how much they want to cling to what they've already got. If they have a well-known name in a particular sector, with a good reputation, they might not want to change. A lot of companies have thrown away one of their biggest advantages by mystifyingly opting to use a different name on the internet.

If, on the other hand, a company's brand needs a spring clean, it might have every reason to want to change. And if it's trying to address a different customer group, that's another reason to change. The Prudential is a well-regarded brand, but it's not exactly dynamic. In order to address a new, younger customer group online, it created an entirely different brand, with a new name, a completely different look, very different marketing and a totally different product offering.

As mentioned earlier, there are also people advantages to both integration and separation. A company may want to preserve its brand heritage; if it has an established brand which is attractive to work for, and a company where the culture is good, it has a big advantage over formless dotcoms with a tiny trading history and a culture defined by the whims of an individual or a small group of people at the top. On the other hand, forming a new company will allow a business to escape from the confines of fixed, ossified corporate structures, which can't change fast enough to attract, keep or accommodate the sort of people it needs to staff your internet operation. They also open up new remuneration options; it may not have to stick with the salary and benefits structures it had in place before.

At a very basic level, the issue of naming is a tricky one. Internet companies have made some poor naming decisions, and so have some established businesses that ought to know better.

Putting .com on the end of your name has the advantage of making it very clear what you do, but it can be restrictive; it marks you out as an internet business, rather than just a business which happens to use the internet as part of what you do. And since the dotcom backlash, when internet shares ceased to be the darlings of the city, it's started to have a few negative connotations.

Far worse are the names with 'e-' or 'i-' or 'cyber' or

'virtual' at the start, or the ones where the letter 'a' has been cleverly morphed into an '@' sign. For the most part, they're just annoying. They're so *internetty*. Companies that use names like these look like they're trying just a little too hard.

The name a company is known by is at the heart of its brand. That's something companies can generally take as read – it's the bedrock of an organization's identity. On the internet, however, even this can be threatened.

No one has an absolute right to a particular name on the net. In many countries, domain names – the whatever.com or .co.uk bits that people use to access your web site – are not anyone's by right. They're bought on the open market. Anyone can reserve them. A lot of the domain registries that sell them don't care who the buyer is; it's not their job to query the buyer's right to a particular name. That has some serious implications both for established businesses seeking to extend what they do onto the internet, and for new players seeking to carve out a niche for themselves.

Increasingly, dotcoms have the problem that good generic names aren't available any more. Any half-memorable word that could be used as a brand name has been bought. What we have now is essentially a resale market; you have to buy a name off someone else who has already bought it. That can be an expensive business.

When jungle.com was launched, for example, the company's founders came up with the name and then tried to buy it from the person who owned it, a computer shop owner on the west coast of the US. When Steve Bennett and his team approached him about the name, he realized he had something that someone else wanted, and promptly set the price at $50,000. Jungle's representatives said they'd have to think about it. Shortly afterwards, they phoned back, saying they'd accept the price. Bad luck, said the vendor – it's now $100,000. They had another think. The price went up again. They eventually paid $235,000, and only managed to get the name legally transferred into their ownership on the day that they launched the new company to the press. This was over a year ago, and the price jungle paid was low. Memorable generic domain names are now regularly sold for seven-figure sums. Companies have recognized the importance of names, and are prepared to pay for the best ones.

MARKETING

The issue for established businesses is slightly different. In the majority of cases, an established company taking its business onto the internet will want to trade there under its established name. So the first hurdle is to work out what the best version of its name is. In the case of Ford, say, ford.com and ford.co.uk look like pretty obvious choices for your global and UK sites. But for a company like Marks & Spencer, should it go for marksandspencer.com, marksandspencer.co.uk, marks-and-spencer.com, marks-and-spencer.co.uk, marks-spencer.com, marks-spencer.co.uk, mands.com, mands.co.uk, m-and-s.com, m-and-s.co.uk, ms.com, ms.co.uk, m-s.com or m-s.co.uk? The company has actually chosen marksandspencer.com. The answer, if you're faced with multiple choices, is to buy all of them and make them point in the direction of the site. But that still means working out which one is going to be promoted as the main address.

The next hurdle is whether your name is available.

Names of well-known companies are valuable, and there are people who make it their business to go around buying them up, with the intention of selling them on. This can be a dubious practice, both ethically and legally. In late 1997 a British company called One in a Million was successfully prosecuted for buying up a number of names of well-known companies, including BT, Marks & Spencer, Virgin, Sainsbury and Ladbroke's, and trying to sell them back to the companies in question. In a case which created a legal precedent in the UK, One in a Million was forced to give the names back.

There are two issues here. One is copyright. If you're Marks & Spencer, surely you have a right to the marksandspencer.com and marksandspencer.co.uk names? But do you have a right to all the possible versions of the name as a web address, listed above? And if my name's Mark, and I set up a computer repair business with my friend Spencer, then perhaps I too have the right to use that name.

The other point is what's known as passing off. Is the holder of the name attempting to profit from the goodwill you've built up around the name? The situation in British law is unclear. If someone holds a version of your name and tries to sell it to you, then technically they've done nothing wrong – they haven't tried to gain from it in any other way. But if they offer to sell it to someone else, or threaten that they're going to do so, they're on much dodgier ground. And it could be argued that the threat to sell the name to someone else is always implicit when they're trying to sell it to you – it's part of what gives the name its value to you. So getting the rights to use what seems to you to be obviously your name may not be as simple as it seems. Resorting to legal channels is expensive, and you may have to weigh that against what the incumbent owner wants for the name, however unreasonable it might sound at first.

Although there are individuals and companies that buy up thousands of domain names with the express intention of selling them on, that doesn't mean that if someone else has your name, or the name you want, they're always going to be a dubious character. For a start, companies in completely separate markets often have identical names. It's not really been an issue before, because, for example, no one's going to confuse the magazine I am editor of, *Revolution*, with Revolution Records or Revolution Road Haulage (they both exist). But on the internet, every company wants to get the domains that are most similar to its name. For UK companies, that generally means the ones that consist of its name with .com and .co.uk on the end. So there can be several companies scrabbling for the same piece of semantic real estate.

If another company with the same name as yours owns a particular domain, you're going to struggle to get it back. Going to court will be messy, costly and unlikely to result in success. A better route, if you can afford it, is to offer to pay the owner for it, but you'll probably have to shell out a pretty generous sum. If a name is already being used for legitimate purposes, the cost to the company selling the name will be high, and it will have to be reimbursed for that. Among other things, it will have to find another suitable name; redirect existing users of its site to a new one; change all of its e-mail addresses; change its stationery, business cards, sales literature, and anywhere else the name is used.

Generic domain names are even more difficult to get hold of. A domain name like travel.com would be great for a travel company, because it's so memorable. But that company would soon find that someone already owns pretty much all the names like this – the ones which describes a particular type of business – as well as the even more generic names like, say, happiness.com or cheap.com. Because there are so many potential buyers for names like these, the cost for people looking to buy them is inevitably going to be very high indeed.

If the situation with regard to domain names is cloudy in British law, then adding in the international dimension makes it murkier still. If someone in another country owns a domain a company thinks it is entitled to (and with .com domains, it's very likely that an American will own them), and they registered it in another country, then whose law is the whole issue of ownership rights decided under? For .com names, some measure of help is at hand. ICANN, the organization in charge of assigning domain names, operates a resolution service, deciding who has the right to own so-called top-level domains (.com, .org and .net), although opinion is varied as to its usefulness. For other domains, no such procedure is in place.

Part of the problem is that very few companies have a consistent name-buying policy. They've just tended to snap up names when it seemed relevant to do so. At the very least, companies need to put the business of administering this whole vital area of intellectual property on a formalized footing.

A brand needs to differentiate a product or service

from its rivals, both online and offline. The brand and its values will need to mark it out as unique, to give people reasons why they should use it rather than any of the proliferating alternatives available to them. Almost by definition, the internet will broaden the competitive landscape, so the task of marking yourself out from the crowd becomes ever more difficult.

The favourite differentiator for internet companies has for a long time been price. There's a mass over-reliance on price as a competitive factor, particularly when it comes to retail, the sector responsible for most advertising of internet-related services. It's a very dangerous road to go down. The internet saves companies money, through decreased overheads: no need for expensive retail premises, each customer order becomes cheaper to process, and so on. And yes, they can pass this on to their customers if they so desire. But then so can everyone else; anyone who operates online should be able to make the same sort of operational savings, and they can pass it on to their customers in exactly the same way, so it ceases to be a differentiator.

There are a number of reasons why so many internet companies compete mainly on price. One is that it's obvious: I'm saving money because I don't have to have expensive physical premises and so on, so I can cut prices. Another is branding colourlessness: I can't think of much else to use as my key brand values, so I'll use price. A third is a lack of confidence: I'll operate my site as a bargain basement because I'm not confident enough that I have a brand which can convince people to pay the sort of premium prices they might to certain real-world companies.

It's tricky to offer a premium-branded and

THE NET EFFECT

premium-priced product or service online. The internet has a wonderful way of finding price anomalies and throwing them back in your face. There isn't the physical distance that you get between real-world retailers – another online shop is only a click away. There's a plethora of shopping portals, with links to multiple products at multiple retailers. If you make a product, it's easy for your customers to see which rival products are cheaper, without the aid of packaging and in-store merchandising to convince people that yours is worth paying for. If you sell, rather than make products, the situation is even more serious: people are one click away from finding out that another retailer is selling the identical product more cheaply. Your plight is becoming even more acute with the rise of price comparison engines and robots, which trawl a selection of sites and find out where you can buy a particular product most cheaply.

It doesn't matter how nicely branded and well designed – on the net, there's really very little to stop someone investigating a product with the excellent information given by one online shop and then buying it 50p cheaper at the really cheap-and-nasty site around the corner. There's very little danger of one of their friends accidentally seeing them in the shop, and they don't have to hold a carrier bag with 'Honest Ron's Discount Supermart' emblazoned on the side while walking down a busy high street. You might be able to differentiate yourself with the ease of the buying interface – people will pay more if it takes them less time. And you might be able to differentiate yourself on trustworthiness and general retailing credibility. But price is a thorny issue. You can't rely on it to mark you out from the competitive crowd, but neither is there likely to be much tolerance of premium-priced sites, unless they add some real value that justifies the extra expense.

It is telling that even Brent Hoberman, founder of lastminute.com, whose site was conceived specifically to exploit price savings and offer bargains, is convinced that price alone is not sufficient to give a brand staying power. By taking products and services from a vast number of suppliers, lastminute.com is able to use the internet's ability to shift perishable inventory like holidays in a short space of time. Because the items would probably have gone unsold and therefore been worthless to the seller, any price is a good price. So lastminute finds itself able to offer goods at knock-down prices.

That's a pretty compelling offer, but lastminute doesn't put it at the core of its brand. It doesn't want to be seen as a bucket shop for low-cost air fares. It doesn't want to be seen as cheap and nasty. It wants to appeal to people's sense of adventure, to reach impulse buyers looking to find a way to treat themselves. That's the direction the presentation of the brand has moved in.

'We can't sell on price alone,' agrees Hoberman. 'We have to sell on customer service, on association with a certain sort of lifestyle. We have to create a community feel. We have to introduce personalization, and improve our customer service that way. It's easy to say, but a lot more difficult to do. But every month we get better at it.'

A couple of other would-be differentiators can fall into the same camp as price – things like speed and convenience. To take retailing as an example again: it's all very well saying that it's quick and easy to buy from you because you're on the web, so people don't have to leave the comfort of their own home/desk, drive to the town centre, park their car and trudge to the shop where they have to stand in a queue for twenty minutes. But once again, that's a claim that anyone who operates on the web can make. You are offering nothing unique.

What this all comes down to is the school of thought that wants to make 'we're on the internet – aren't we something?' its key selling point. It's roughly akin to imagining that 'we have shops' is a devastating brand proposition. It isn't, and it never will be. Being on the internet is not big, and it's not clever. There are certain characteristics that all web sites have, and you cannot try and use them as selling points. Trying to do so is like a greengrocer's shop promoting itself by advertising the fact that buying runner beans there is easier than growing your own.

'Things like speed and customer service are the minimum basis on which you compete,' comments Ernesto Schmidt of Peoplesound.com. 'You have to find other ways of differentiating yourself.'

His own company's first advertising campaign fell into the trap of advertising itself solely as a place to get music on the internet, nothing that a lot of other sites don't offer. It appeared to be an example of exactly the sort of bad dotcom advertising that doesn't seek to establish a proper brand proposition, instead relying on just shouting the name lots of times very loudly, together with a few vague statements that it's great because it's on the internet. According to Schmidt, however, this is deliberate – an attempt to get the peoplesound name planted in the public imagination, before a second wave of publicity to establish brand specifics in the minds of consumers. Following the initial 'music free you' blast, the company concentrated for a long time on reaching music industry professionals and opinion-formers with targeted advertising and PR, before moving into a second wave of mass-marketing to build a brand with meaning, which is all about the ability of each individual to choose music they like and get hold of it for free.

'People are confused, because there are fifty million music web sites out there,' says Schmidt. 'That's why we've pushed the fact that we are Europe's biggest very hard. We've really pounded that, as a credibility building exercise. Now we've done that, we'll be concentrating on building brand emotions.

'We had to make sure that we were 100 per cent happy with the product before we moved into the second phase of our advertising. We deliberately held back on the campaign until we were sure that it was absolutely right. You can't try and convince consumers that the product is right if you're not convinced yourself.'

Online book retailer BOL initially fell into the trap of using characteristics it shares with most of its competitors as its differentiators in its advertising. When the company launched in the UK, it embarked on a famously bad ad campaign, which it ran across outdoor and public transport: 'The new British bookshop on the internet.' Quite apart from the fact that BOL (owned by media giant Bertelsmann) is very clearly German, the campaign really does prompt the question: why? Why would I go there? What is it about this ad that makes me abandon Amazon.com, or even the high-street bookshop down the road and use BOL? The answer is: nothing. I do not care whether something is new or not, unless that newness offers some kind of tangible benefit contingent on its novelty; in fact, with a retailer, most people are more likely to trust an old, established name. I am not jingoistic enough to care that the shop is British (even when it actually isn't), and I'd wager that very few of the book-buying public are either. The fact that it's a bookshop prompts the response: we already have bookshops. What is going to make me go to this one rather than the ones I already know and trust? And 'on the internet' makes me think, what's so great about that? What benefits does being on the internet offer me as a prospective buyer? And aren't those things that are already offered by the numerous other bookshops on the internet. Why is this one better?

To be fair to BOL, it has since cleaned up its act with a campaign it ran during late 1999 and early 2000 based around the proposition of loving books, and people who do so coming to BOL. It still makes me wonder why that marks it out from other book retailers, whose customers presumably also love books, but the point of differentiation from the company's main online competitor, Amazon, is clear – Amazon sells more or less everything these days. BOL wants to communicate that it is as passionate about books as the hardcore book-lovers it has singled out as its main target audience. The problem is that there's not much you can get from BOL that you can't get from Amazon, or from many of its other competitors – it's differentiating itself by what it's not rather than by what it is, by what it doesn't sell rather than what it does sell. And it doesn't do much to put clear water between BOL and its more upmarket offline competitors like Waterstone's. But the love of books does have a resonant emotional appeal. It works to differentiate the BOL brand from, say, WHSmith. As Broich points out, serious book lovers would be reluctant to go there to buy their books, even if they were available there. It just isn't the brand experience they want.

BOL's most intelligent marketing efforts have been online. In late 1999, it ran the 'Happy Hour' promotion, where for an hour it gave anyone visiting its site and registering a free book. It followed this up in spring 2000 with a similar campaign, in which anyone buying a book could send a free one to a friend.

Giving your core product away for free might sound like commercial suicide, but there's sound thinking behind the move. The gamble BOL took was based on the cost of customer acquisition. It costs a lot of marketing money to get a customer to come and buy, far more than the price of a book. If the price of a book alone was enough to get people to use the site, then it might be enough to convince them of the site's virtues, and tie them into a cycle of convenience-driven repeat buying. That's the theory, at least. Even if people just picked up their freebie and didn't come back, they'd registered at the site, so BOL knew who they were, knew all about them, knew what sort of books they liked, and could target them with future promotions and offers. It certainly had a better chance of turning each one of them into a committed customer than it had had before it ran the campaign. And the PR value of giving books away for free got the company far more publicity than another billboard campaign could ever have done.

It's not only the thinking behind campaigns that

can be deficient. You can also get the opposite: a reasonably well thought out proposition, accompanied by the most appalling creative treatment. AOL, for example, had clearly thought long and hard about who its customers were, and tried to target them with an appropriate message. It was talking to families, and it would therefore advertise based on values like trustworthiness, reliability, security and flexibility. The result was a truly horrible campaign. It featured 'Connie', a young woman in a shimmery silvery dress who came out of the family in the ad's computer screen and told them about all the wonderful things they could do with AOL. She was presumably supposed to be bright and bouncy, with an unthreatening family-orientated appeal. I know this is a subjective judgement, and I'm probably not in AOL's target market, but she was the most annoying single thing in the world, ever. An obnoxious chirpiness combined with a schoolmarmish prissiness and a would-be chumminess, and remote controls were thrown at TV screens up and down the land. It was the UK's first big TV campaign for a mass-market internet brand, and as such it got a lot of publicity. At that time, there wasn't the same need to rush to get on TV that most internet companies' ads seem to suffer from these days, and the ad had clearly had some thought put into it. But it set a template of creative mediocrity that the industry has yet to get over.

The early 2000 TV and cinema ad campaign for Freeserve may not have suffered from creative mediocrity in its execution, but it had as bad a problem: the supposed brand values weren't linked to brand experience. AOL's campaign thought about the experience of using the service and how to build brand values out of it, but the ads themselves were terrible. Freeserve's campaign seemed to be based on a branding exercise which had come up with a collection of brand values in a vacuum, completely divorced from the service itself.

The campaign featured disabled model Aimee Mullins. It had her talking about her experiences, set against images of her doing her work, in a way which emphasized brand values of freedom, individuality and innovation. The problem was that it appeared to the viewer (at least to this viewer) to have absolutely nothing to do with Freeserve. The viewer has no idea what the campaign is about until the end, when the word 'free' appeared on the screen, changing into the Freeserve logo. An inspiring ad, yes, but what did it have to do with anyone's experience of using Freeserve, which is, after all, an ISP service with a big portal site full of all sorts of different content attached to it? The ad had the impression of being based purely on an aspirational brand positioning – what the brand wanted to be, rather than what it actually was. Simply stating brand values and expecting people to believe them and identify with them is not enough. People have to experience them when they use the product or service.

It's one area where having a physical dimension to a brand can be a big advantage, and where established companies can score over new players. If there's a physical item or space that people can pick up or go into, they have a tangible experience of what a brand stands for. They have their own feelings about that brand, which can be reinforced in the way it is marketed. Internet-only players, or companies that want to create new and different brands for their internet presences, are forced to create brand values from a non-tangible, two-dimensional experience which at the moment is frequently uninspiring in the extreme; the temptation is to fall back on the obvious, the price-speed-convenience axis, because there's often very little else to draw on.

The AOL and Freeserve ads may have been bad, but at least they didn't try to come across all wacky and crazy. The tyranny of 'fun' internet ads, based on groan-making puns delivered by D-list celebrities with the kind of irony that thinks it makes mediocrity acceptable but actually fails completely to do so, is something the internet community has to get over if it wants its advertising to become truly memorable and truly effective.

My favourite example, first highlighted in the US edition of my magazine (*Revolution US*, June 2000, p.51), is Webex, a company that provides online service to streamline business meetings. The company promotes itself with ads using celebrity transvestite Ru Paul, alongside the slogan: 'Meetings used to be such a drag'. It's a weak and obvious pun. More to the point, it has nothing to do with the product. The same pun on the word drag could be applied to any internet product or service, or indeed to any product or service. Not only does it fail to differentiate itself from other similar services, it fails to differentiate itself from anything. It's just about the ultimate example of the minor-celebrity-and-pun school of dotcom advertising. If internet ads are going to start meaning anything to people, this stuff has got to stop.

Yet another bear-trap is the good ad for a bad product. If a company doesn't have complete confidence in its web site, it shouldn't open it up to the cruel glare of its customers. Running a high-profile ad campaign is the surest way to highlight its weakness. Even if a company does have complete confidence in its online offering, it should take a deep breath before embarking on a big advertising push. The founders of boo.com, for instance, obviously had confidence in their product, hence their decision to run ads when they did, and on the scale they did.

The ads themselves were quite entertaining – a load of geeks taking over a basketball court to the bemusement of the other players, or the same people doing exercises on a crowded subway train, surrounded by nonplussed fellow passengers. But they betrayed a certain schizophrenia. Boo was supposed to be drop-dead cool, the place really trendy, aspirational people shopped on the net. It was supposed to be the antithesis of everything that catalogue shopping – the direct antecedent of online retailing – was all about. But the message sent out by boo's campaign was that you didn't have to be cool to buy this stuff – it was open to everyone, because anyone could use the site. It tried to be cutting-edge and cool, which by its nature means exclusive, but also mass-market. The ads reflected that confusion about its own identity. They were undoubtedly enjoyable, but the strategy behind them was flawed. They held up a mirror to most of the advertising for internet-related enterprises pretty accurately: the time hadn't been put in to think through the proposition properly, to really position the brand, to give it values, benefits, differentiators.

It's a shame, because boo was a laudable attempt to create an online brand with a bit of personality, a splash of colour. Most people's experiences of most web sites – and this is particularly true of sites whose main aim is to sell things – are disappointing. The sites are functional, lacking in fizz or sparkle, without colour. There's none of the tangibility of brand experience that you get with a good physical retail brand. Think of the breathtaking size and grandeur of a top department store, the feeling of excitement and exclusivity you get from a chic clothing boutique, or the mouthwatering aromas and tantalizing displays you'll find in a good food retailer. What the founders of boo got right was to realize that they needed to create something different from the run-of-the-mill internet experience, something which matched the best offline brands. Selling clothes in particular, and fashionable clothes at that, required a bit more oomph, a bit more character, a bit more showbiz. That, in many ways, was what the whole boo experience was all about. It was why it was so ambitious, and it was ultimately why it failed. The company overstretched itself. It had the odds stacked against it from the start, trying to sell a product like clothes, which people like to pick up, feel, and maybe try on before buying. The way in which it went about trying to build a brand meant it had even more of an uphill struggle, and the way cash flowed out of the company as it attempted to do so was a big factor in its eventual downfall.

The blanket blitz of hopeless offline advertising for online services really got into gear and started swamping media outlets across the board in late 1999, when dotcom mania was at its height. With the stock market correction of early 2000 and the shakeout among internet-only players that began with the closure of boo.com, the hyper-acceleration of internet advertising slowed to more sensible levels. Companies realized that so many of their campaigns were full of sound and fury but brought them very little long-term value. They were costing a lot of money, it was difficult to achieve stand-out, and a lot of them were built on sand. It became apparent that this was not the most cost-effective way to build a company.

This would be fine, if another tool in the marketing arsenal were not stepping into its place as the knee-jerk promotional mechanism of choice for internet companies: PR. Getting a company lots of press coverage can make it very visible among consumers, other business and potential employees alike. It's tempting to try to get your company's name in the press as many times as you possibly can, particularly if you are trying to raise investment. The more of a name it can build up for itself as a smart operator with an innovative business, the more likely it is to be able to attract the attention of potential investors. And PR seems pretty cheap by comparison with ads: retain the services of a smart PR company for a few thousand a month. It's not too much of a risk – if you don't get for your company the exposure it's after, you can always sack them and get another.

But PR can be as unthinking a tool as advertising, if it's used badly. The danger lies in over-exposing a company to the public glare before it's really ready for it. Not all publicity is good publicity, and the more a company gets, the more likely it is to be leapt on and savaged by the media, particularly in the UK, with the build-'em-up-to-knock-'em-down culture of the press here. If people have had a company thrust down their throats, they will try and pick holes in what it does. If they're bored with hearing about it and feel that it's been hyped, it's in for a very rough ride indeed. As with advertising, a high profile is all very well, but it has to have some kind of grounding in the reality of what a company actually does.

Already PR companies, in particular the specialist internet ones, are experiencing the same spiralling growth rates as other types of company in the internet economy. I speak to several who have more or less given up going out and actively pitching for accounts, who have to turn away work because they can't service it, who can't find the people they need however hard they try. They're experiencing this kind of rapid expansion precisely because, if they're any good, accounts are just falling into their lap; everyone has heard that they need a big PR campaign, in exactly the same way as everyone has heard that they need a big advertising campaign. The danger is when this isn't a considered decision.

If they're not careful, they face exactly the same problems of rapid expansion as anyone else – a loss of focus, a dilution of the quality of their people, the need to find ever more innovative ways of promoting their clients. If these problems impact on the quality of the work they do, they become problems for their clients as well.

The founders of boo.com must have started off thinking that there was no such thing as bad PR, or indeed as too much PR. The company was leapt on when it was first publicized in the spring of 1999 as the perfect example of the buoyant new economy. The project was ambitious; the company had unheard-of levels of funding, eventually amounting to £130m, which would have been generous for a US company, let alone a European one; the company was funky and trendy, selling cool gear through a sexily-designed site; its founders were young and photogenic; and what's more they had that rarest of things, experience of running a successful internet company, Scandanavian online book retailer bokus.com, which they'd sold a couple of years previously. All these things helped to create a furious hype around the company. It was popular with the specialist internet press, but it was also popular with the lifestyle press, the preferred reading material of its target audience. Before the company had even launched, a series of excited, breathy articles focused lovingly on its size, its trendiness, the number of employees, the uniquely relaxed and motivated staff, the sheer breathtaking ambition of the whole thing. The company's PR machine had done its job very well. It made a huge number of people aware of the brand, many of whom went to have a look. And it must have done wonders for the company's profile among investors.

Things started to go wrong when the company failed to launch on schedule. Articles started to appear ridiculing the incompetence of this company that had spent a fortune on advertising, salaries and other overheads, and couldn't even manage to launch its site on time (I wrote one or two myself). The people who had read and heard all about the site visited it and found it wasn't open for business; their experience was disappointing, in exactly the same way as the experience of the people who had seen the company's ads and gone to visit the site was disappointing. As time dragged on and the site still didn't launch, the laughing-stock status of boo started to grow. And rather than turn off the PR tap, the machine carried on inexorably, doing its aggressive promotional thing.

It all reached its apogee when an article about catalogue shopping appeared in a leading men's lifestyle magazine. The piece purported to be testing out different catalogue shops through the experiences of readers of the magazine. One of the catalogues in question was online – it was boo.com. The reader in question was pictured, sitting among a collection of brightly-coloured boo.com boxes, waxing lyrical about how he always bought from boo, and found the service excellent. All good publicity for the brand, then, except for one key fact: boo hadn't launched yet.

This was PR overkill at its most extreme. Not just hyping a service, but hyping a service that didn't even exist yet. As the launch delay lengthened, boo took its place as the dotcom whipping boy, the one everyone laughed at. Even before it became fashionable to knock internet companies, boo was the school spanner, the fat kid with no mates, the one it was OK to hate. It was a role it was to have right up until it went under. Stories of boo's failings proliferated. Some were completely apocryphal. The amount of money the company had received in investment seemed to grow by £10m every time you heard it. A rumour did the rounds that the site would not accept returns of unwanted goods – in fact, surveys regularly found its fulfilment and customer service to be among the best of any European web site. But that didn't matter. Boo had a massive 'kick me' sign all of its own devising hung round its neck. It had hyped itself and then failed to deliver the goods, and so everyone laughed at it. You could make a strong argument that they laughed it out of existence.

Similarly, lastminute.com was riding for a fall the moment co-founder Martha Lane Fox started appearing on *Newsnight* and *Question Time* as a spokesman for the dotcom generation. The company didn't even have to go as far as boo.com and actually fail, to find itself on the receiving end of a barrage of derision. The founders of lastminute.com, Lane Fox and her business partner Brent Hoberman, were promoted very aggressively and very successfully, first among the business press, and then to a wider consumer audience. The company became widely known as an exciting young British success story: it was heralded as one of the players shaping this brave new economy, with a business that couldn't have existed without the net and an entrepreneurial zeal rare in the UK, which typified the fearless breaking down of traditional business boundaries that the internet hailed.

When the company's share price started to fall, soon after it was floated, they were widely leapt on and slated in the media as young, foolish dreamers, with no solid foundation for their business, young upstarts who were getting their comeuppance. The admiring articles in the national press about envy of the personal wealth of young internet entrepreneurs soon gave way to excited chattering about weaknesses in lastminute's fundamental business model, a lot of it fuelled by jealousy, which gave way to schadenfreude as the share price fell post-float. It descended to the level of petty personal carping at the expense of Lane Fox. The tabloids followed her around and tried to dredge up dirt from her past. The internet industry itself was gripped by bright green envy, followed by smugness. Mainstream media outlets saw the company as their legitimate prey. Lane Fox had been everywhere, and that made her the ideal target to slag

MARKETING

off. As lastminute's share price tumbled, so the volume of abuse rose. The company's founders had been venerated as the vanguard of the bright new young things who were going to reshape the economy; now everyone was sick of them sounding off about the new economy, while they ran a company that didn't come close to making a profit and had seen its share price tumble.

PR is a valuable tool, and it can be a cost-effective way of getting a company's name well known. But the media is an unpredictable beast; it can be fantastically beneficial to have it on your side, but at any moment it might bite you. At least you can control the message sent out by your advertising. Using the goodwill of journalists in the written and broadcast media to your advantage is always a good idea, but beware. It might be cheaper than other forms of marketing, but it's also a lot more unstable.

It is in the nature of brands that they stretch, that they develop to include new elements. If a brand is known and liked and trusted, it makes sense to use it in as many different ways as possible, to exploit its profile and popularity. The classic example of this is Virgin, a brand which has been stretched from its original business of music retail to include, among others, air travel, train travel, alcoholic and soft drinks, music publishing, financial services and telecoms. The brand had certain key attributes of value, accessibility, friendliness and a certain maverick quality, most of them residing in its founder Richard Branson, which allowed it to extend what it does across such an apparently disparate range of products and services.

Internet-related brands are particularly keen to rid

themselves of their association with one particular product and use their brand more widely. The shortage of strong, well-known brands with a heritage means that those which are well known and have built up certain characteristics in the eyes of their users are keen to extend what they do. It's also relatively easy for a company to expand its product range in the virtual world, because it doesn't have to go through the tiresome business of acquiring more expensive retail space.

Amazon.com, for example, which started off selling just books, now also sells music, which is a fairly obvious brand extension; consumer electronics goods, which is slightly less obvious; and antiques, which isn't obvious at all. In fact, the company now owns a stake in auction house Sotheby's, while the world's biggest online auction company, eBay, actually bought out US auction house Butterfields. Similarly, where Software Warehouse sold computer software and peripherals, jungle.com now sells books, music and videos as well.

The danger for companies that stretch their brands is that they go too far, too fast, and end up falling flat on their faces. Amazon may one day find that it has come up against its very own Virgin Trains, and face the problem of the service being unable to live up to the brand's promises, either explicitly spelt out by marketing, or implicitly held in the values which are understood to belong to that brand from the existing services it offers.

Different types of product and service have different requirements in terms of customer service, logistics and fulfilment, buying interface, and all sorts of other things. Companies that try and do everything can end up losing focus and doing those things badly.

They can actually end up damaging the very brand which allowed them to expand. As ever, it's a matter of moving at the right speed, planning well in advance, and understanding which particular new product or service areas the brand is suited to. Just because extending the range of products and services it offers is relatively easy for a company to do on the internet, that doesn't mean it should necessarily do it. In reality, any company from any background could at any point in time decide that it wanted to stretch to include more or less anything else. This is not just an internet thing. The truth is that most of the time, companies aren't busy expanding what they do; they're trying to do what they do well, and they may occasionally extend it if it seems relevant.

At the height of the unsustainable economic boom of the 1980s there was similar brand stretch frenzy; at one point, advertising agency Saatchi and Saatchi, for example, which had flourished in the boom, was rumoured to be interested in buying a high-street bank. An extreme example, but it illustrates how things can get taken too far. The company would not have been set up in any way to handle the business of running a bank, and just because a company operates mainly on the internet, that doesn't make it any more able to cross huge divides.

People tend to identify certain brands with certain products or services. Whatever else it sells, Amazon is still thought of by most people as a book retailer first and foremost, and jungle as a retailer of computer-related products, which at the time of writing made up 80 per cent of its revenues.

Given that so many web sites make their money by

accepting advertising, it is surprising that the internet itself hasn't proved more popular among internet companies trying to promote themselves to potential customers. Recently, most of the marketing of internet brands has used mass-market, offline media like TV and posters. While advertising online might be good for targeting certain customer groups, your potential audience is limited to people who have already got some form of internet access. Besides, the creative restrictions of a letter-box shaped banner ad on a web site make it a far less attractive option when you're trying to get a brand message across than a 30-second TV commercial, a page in a magazine or a huge billboard. When companies feel that they need speed to market, the mass-market campaign looks like a pretty good way to get it.

None the less, if the internet is used intelligently, it can still be a very effective way of promoting an online venture. This need for intelligence applies both to the media placement and to the creative execution. In exactly the same way as offline media campaigns, a load of banner ads randomly splashed around a few high-traffic locations are unlikely to achieve anything very concrete; identifying a target audience and advertising in places they visit is likely to be more effective. That can take the form of partnerships as much as advertising. If a company sells, say, fashion, it might want to link up with a music retailer, so that people can click back and forth between the two sites. It's a simple idea, but it can pay dividends.

The way in which advertising on the net motivates people to click, and then to buy, is a complex issue and one that no one has resolved. The creative executions of banners on web sites were traditionally simple and direct. If a company sold books, it found sites which it thought keen book-buyers might visit, and it placed ads on them saying something along the lines of 'Books – click here'. The idea was that banner ads encouraged response, but they weren't much use for building brand values. The problem is that without really meaningful branding to give people a reason to click, very few of them did. Most people know where they can get books on the internet, so why would they respond to a banner ad that didn't give them any reason to choose that particular online bookshop? Clickthrough rates – the number of people who clicked on an ad, expressed as a percentage of the total number who were exposed to it – just kept falling. Around half a per cent is now pretty much standard. Given that most advertisers pay for how many people view their ad, rather than how many click on it, this is a problem, and is one explanation for the unpopularity of banners relative to other types of media.

It doesn't tell the whole story, though. Just because the response rate to a banner can be measured, that doesn't mean it should be the only figure used to evaluate the success, or otherwise, of a campaign. Online advertising can have an effect on brand, but so far, most of the ads designed for the internet haven't had that as their main aim. Ernesto Schmidt of Peoplesound.com is a firm believer that online ads should aim to be creative, and build brand values. 'We looked at online advertising in some detail in an attempt to answer the question, what works and what doesn't?' he comments. 'The banners that don't work are those that tell you what a site is and what it does. They're the traditional form of online advertising, and they're the ones that get 0.5 per cent clickthrough. The ones that work are those that appeal to the deadly sins: greed, curiosity, lust etc. We need to stop thinking of banners as an information window and start thinking about them as a way to entice people. The clickthrough rate always comes down to the creative that you use.'

Once a company has run a campaign, it needs to know what works and what doesn't. This sounds pretty obvious, but it's amazing how often it isn't done. In the world of scattergun internet marketing, where no one knows what works and so everyone tries a bit of everything, splashing their ads over TV, newspapers, magazines, radio, posters, buses, bus shelters, taxis and underground trains, it isn't easy to work out which, if any, is having any effect, and which is the most effective. Especially as advertising isn't the only marketing weapon in your arsenal – if you can't compare the effectiveness of say, a TV ad or a poster ad, how can you compare the effectiveness of a TV ad, a direct mail campaign, or a poster ad and a targeted e-mail promotion? And if companies don't identify the most effective ways to market themselves to their potential customers, then they are going to carry on wasting money on ineffective executions, without being able to do anything about it.

Steve Bennett of jungle.com is particularly scathing about the lack of research done by internet companies, and in particular those in the retail sector, into the effectiveness of their advertising.

'It stuns me that you can go onto the top ten e-tailing sites in the UK, and none of them, with the exception of ours, asks you where you found out about it,' he says. 'It's the most basic principle of direct marketing, but people aren't doing it. They're taking a totally scattergun marketing approach, but they're not trying to find out what works, so no one knows.'

Asking people directly where they found out about a service is not the only way to track the effectiveness of various marketing executions. A company could include a different web address, pointing to a different page, on each ad that it runs, or running ads in rotation and inferring the effectiveness of each one from variations in traffic. In certain circumstances, the 'where did you hear about this site' approach might look a bit naff. If you have a brand which aspires to be more upscale, exclusive or premium-priced than the intensely mass-market jungle.com, it might not seem appropriate. You probably won't want to make your customers go through the irritating business of having to give you that information, but be aware that if you make it optional, the data you collect might not be reliable, or the sample might not be big enough to be statistically robust. That doesn't mean that companies shouldn't research the effectiveness of their marketing, just that they should think carefully about how they do it.

A lot of money is spent acquiring customers. Once they have been acquired, they have to be kept. Whatever market a company operates in, there's no point in spending a lot of money to get someone to visit its site, if they visit once and then never come back. Mass-market advertising can't guarantee repeat custom. Relying too much on customers coming back for repeat visits is a good way to justify inappropriately high customer acquisition costs. If a company can't guarantee that it can keep its customers, it's throwing its money away.

Developing relationships with customers, by giving them something which they perceive to be of value, is the key to keeping them coming back. Simply communicating with existing customers can be incredibly valuable. If a company knows enough about its customers to be able to send them relevant information about products, and has their permission to do so, that can make them feel valued and stimulate them to buy again, particularly if the offer is phrased as some form of promotion. It's those regular customers that need nurturing with targeted and highly specific marketing, because they're the ones that will give a company the bulk of its business. It can mean taking it as far as personalizing their experience and delivering something that appears to be tailored for them; but be aware that this can be difficult, and getting it wrong can be massively counter-productive. However, personalization takes a lot of forms, and some of them are fairly risk-free.

Jungle.com, for example, encourages its customers to sign up to receive e-mails from the company. Each customer can select which types of product they want to be e-mailed about, and determine how regularly they want to receive the e-mail, so that they're not bombarded with more communication than they want to receive. According to the company's managing director Steve Bennett, it's the second highest generator of custom for the company, and it's far and away the most cost-efficient. He wants to make it the main way of driving custom to the site in the future, and expects the cost of customer acquisition to drop to reflect that.

*

Marketing is a tool – a complex tool. But the point of marketing is to deliver results. Its role is to build a brand and acquire customers. Ultimately, it has to be measured against the bottom line. It is not a clever way to spend lots of money; it is an investment rather than a cost.

All obvious stuff, but it needs saying, because so many internet companies have flagrantly ignored it. Marketing is more than a lever you push when you want to grow; it is a delicate and much-misunderstood mechanism.

There is no point in marketing a bad product. Advertising is just one option. Billboards are just one type of advertising. Too many internet companies fail to understand this. Mass-market advertising is not the best route for everyone. Ads that fail to market a brand out from the crowd are useless.

The majority of ads for internet services mean nothing to most of the people that see them. They're irrelevant and, a lot of the time, quite irritating. It's not like the offline world, where people already have an internal map of brands and can decode the advertising of a new one, albeit often subconsciously, and work out where it fits into the overall scheme of things. Most people are familiar with no more than a handful of internet companies, if they're familiar with any at all. They need to understand what something does, and they need to understand what the benefit of using it is to them.

The internet offers companies a unique chance to get inside the heads of their customers, find out what makes them tick and exploit that. This is the sort of thing that traditional marketing techniques have always been a very distant means to the end of doing.

It's slightly dismaying that, faced with such an opportunity, so many companies fall back on lazy, expensive, ill-targeted, ineffective marketing.

CHAPTER SIX

COMPETITORS, SUPPLIERS AND PARTNERS

The internet changes the competitive landscape, and that landscape is constantly evolving. The arrival of new players is bound to shake up any market. But it goes deeper than there just being a few new competitors to worry about.

New players may do the same thing as incumbents, but do it far more efficiently, or just differently. Markets will become increasingly Darwinian. Everyone is fixated on first-mover advantage and the benefits it can bring. But no one is safe – businesses will find that new competitors are constantly springing up, and some of them will be companies they've never heard of, or at least never viewed as a competitor before. Just as established businesses may move into sectors they've never been in before and find themselves competing with each other in ways they never previously did, so companies may find themselves working with other organizations they'd previously thought of as competitors. Ford, General Motors and Daimler-Chrysler, the three biggest motor manufacturers in the US, now have a common web-based purchasing platform to deal with suppliers.

Organizations' relationships with other companies – whether they be competitors, business partners or suppliers – are going to change. In this context, it is vitally important for a business to know exactly who its competitors are, both online and offline, and to have a realistic sense of what the competition is up to, how strong it is, and how well it can deal with it. It's a tricky and labour-intensive process, because some of these competitors will almost certainly come from unexpected quarters. And it's a continuous process, because the nature of the competition changes constantly.

Charcol Online is a case in point. John Charcol is a market leader in the physical world, where its nearest competitors are companies like Saville's and Chase DeVere. As mentioned earlier, the service these companies offer – comparing a range of mortgage offers to find the best one for a particular individual – is the sort of thing the internet does very well. So it's natural to expect a few new companies to make a play for that space.

Toby Strauss, managing director of Charcol Online, says the company has to be constantly vigilant. 'We look all the time at who our competitors are. One of the best ways to find out is to talk to our lenders about who else is approaching them.' Several internet-only players have entered Charcol's space. They include E-LOAN and MoneySupermarket, along with broader services like MoneyExtra, which gives its users various product and supplier options across a range of different personal finance categories. There's also Netmortgage, which is backed by Charcol's biggest offline competitor Saville's, but operates under the separate online brand. Most of the

207

COMPETITORS,
SUPPLIERS AND
PARTNERS

company's other big offline competitors didn't have any meaningful online presence at the time of writing.

Strauss believes the incumbents can take the lead online; first-mover advantage isn't solely the preserve of nimble-footed dotcoms. 'The likes of E-LOAN launched relatively late in the UK, and we moved faster than our bricks and mortar equivalents in the US,' he says. 'We're an established company that has taken a leading position online. You see it happen in other markets as well: egg is the leading online bank, and that's part of a very traditional organization.'

The arrival of new players in the online mortgage brokering market is in stark contrast to its offline counterpart, which is pretty static and unchanging. Many of the barriers to entry that prevent new players challenging the big offline brokers aren't there on the web. The cost of physical premises is an obvious example. Several of the online players also cut costs by reducing the amount of admin they're responsible for. Several simply provide leads to mortgage providers rather than taking care of all the mortgage administration themselves, through one central process which applies whichever lender a customer chooses – the route that the traditional players like Charcol take. Although the internet makes it easier for new players to enter the market, they still have the problem of low brand recognition, and established players have a big advantage in the shape of their relationships with lenders. They're far more likely to get exclusive products to offer to their customers, because they've been working with the lenders for a long time and the lenders understand the value they bring.

The online service has also helped to bring John Charcol closer to the lenders it deals with. It's a business which is 100 per cent reliant upon the participation of those suppliers: they provide the product that the company presents to consumers. The more lenders John Charcol gets on board, the stronger its consumer proposition becomes. Charcol Online has also gone out of its way to explain its proposition to lenders; it had to, if it wanted to build up a good range of products to offer its customers. That's had a beneficial effect on its relationships with the lenders. They're starting to realize that Charcol is a valuable source of business to them, particularly Charcol Online, which takes a lot of the administrative work away from them and more or less hands them customers on a plate.

'The lenders have been pretty positive about it,' says Strauss. 'A couple have even said to me in private that it's given their board a wake-up call. They've traditionally been very sceptical about the value of the internet, except as a pure advertising medium. A lot of them have now started working on back-end systems that will allow them to take mortgage applications electronically.

'Our financial relationships with our suppliers are the same as offline, and we're currently considering whether they should be. In the old world, business that they get through an intermediary is much more difficult for them to process, but that's not the case online, so us going online is an advantage for them which perhaps ought to be reflected in our commercial relationships with them. We're working with lenders to try and work out how they can recompense us for the work we've put in. They're generally pretty unsophisticated in their approach, so a change like that needs long-term explanation. But they're actually beginning to help us now. For the first time, they're thinking to themselves: "Maybe we should be nice to those guys."'

'We had a party when we launched Charcol Online, and we invited all the lenders,' he adds. 'One of them came up to me and said: "That's the first time I've ever been bought a drink by an intermediary."'

Britannica is in the unusual position of being an incumbent in one market – paper encyclopaedias – but a newcomer in another. In its new incarnation as a media company, it finds itself competing with a lot of very well established media businesses. Also, curiously, it finds itself competing with a huge number of internet-only media-based companies. So the nature of its competition has completely changed. Not so long ago, it was other publishers of paper encyclopaedias. Then it became the likes of Encarta. Now, at the very least, it's every business that sells advertising on the internet; but it could equally be seen as every business that sells advertising on any medium.

'Let's be frank,' says the company's UK managing director Jason Plent. 'We want to steal some traffic. Bricks and mortar companies do have assets that will enable them to compete with the new players, and I'm fairly certain that we can be one of them.'

Britannica's direct competition will be the major web portals, the likes of Yahoo, Excite, Lycos and MSN (so it's still up against Microsoft). Those are the companies its product offering will compete with, and those are the companies it will compete most directly with for ad revenue. But monitoring who constitutes the competition will be a continuous challenge for the company; in a few short years, it's gone from having a handful of competitors to potentially millions.

Competition from all sides is something Marks & Spencer has long had to face. In a sense, everyone's a competitor for the company, because it sells so many different types of product that there's some crossover with more or less every other retailer. But, in another sense, no one competes with the company, because there's no other retailer that can match its range, and none that comes close to occupying quite the same universally trusted niche in the shopping psyche of the British consumer. The company's head of e-commerce Peter Robinson is adamant that the internet isn't about to move the company from this unique position – if anything, it will increase the range of products the company can sell, and allow it to compete in even more areas. 'Other people growing their businesses affects us, but only in small sectors of what we do,' he says. 'We serve 76 per cent of the UK population every month, and have a massive share of so many markets. We have 14 to 15 per cent of the entire ladieswear market in the UK, and between 30 and 40 per cent of the lingerie market.

'New competition comes around more rapidly than people think when you have that breadth of offering. If you look at all the growth markets at the moment, in areas like consumer electronics or mobile phones, we might not sell those things, but there's an issue with share of wallet going into other markets and being diverted from the products we sell. So it all affects us.

'But what we've got that's so incredibly powerful is this brand that everyone believes in. We could sell everything, from a pint of milk to a mobile phone to a loan.' Even in markets where the company is completely dominant, it's prepared to look at the competitive landscape in new ways online. As Robinson points out, M&S has a massive share of the UK lingerie market, but rather than believing that it can simply transplant its offline success onto the internet and dominate there as well, it has decided to partner with other companies where it's relevant for it to do so. Through its investment arm, the company has a share in splendour.com, an online lingerie retailer. The company decided to partner with another business, which could have been seen as a competitor, and actually to invest in it to form new brands which can help it reach different customer groups and have a stronger, broader appeal online. The idea is for the main M&S web site to link through to splendour.com; it's rather like an in-store concession, something which M&S hasn't done before.

For M&S, it's a matter of being selective about partnerships. Robinson says he receives a lot of approaches, and only rarely does anything come of them. 'You wouldn't believe the number of people who come to us, pleading for us to partner with them,' he says. 'People who partner with us have an opportunity to promote themselves to 14 million customers a week, to our 6.2 million charge card holders, to the 2.8 million people who read our customer magazine, and on our shopfronts, bags and so on.

'We don't see ourselves as being an island. As a multi-channel retailer, we will be using other routes to broaden our offering and promote what we do more widely. That probably means identifying partners to help us build our brand, but they have to be the right partners.'

It's not just established businesses that are forced to continually reassess whom they compete with. Dotcoms know only too well that it's possible for new players to spring up in their market at any time – it's what they did themselves. Ernesto Schmidt at Peoplesound.com says it's vital that his company does regular research in order to determine who its competitors are. It's part of what he calls 'being like a real business. It's the sort of thing you'd expect the likes of P&G to do,' he enthuses. Peoplesound operates in a crowded area with numerous sites offering music for download. Some make their money from advertising; some sell merchandise and tickets; some charge for the music, either per track or by subscription; some act as a kind of virtual agent, helping artists find a record label; some take money from major labels in return for giving them a platform where they can test out new acts; many combine several or all of these revenue streams. Peoplesound, which makes the bulk of its money from selling custom CDs of music to people after allowing them to hear a selection of tracks for free online, needs to identify which of those sites are competitors and which aren't.

'If you're in the restaurant business, you can define yourself against everything from McDonald's to Le Caprice,' Ernesto Schmidt says. 'Similarly, as a site featuring downloadable music, we can define ourselves against everything from MP3.com to musicunsigned.com to iCrunch. We need to identify which of those we think are real competitors. We think the likes of iCrunch will fall out because they don't have any content, they're just an online version of HMV. So they're going to be eaten for breakfast, lunch and dinner by the established retailers; that's who the record companies are going to give content to, because they have established relationships with them. Other sites, like MP3.com, are just huge unregulated communities. In a way, it's easy for us. Getting blank CDs and blank boxes, putting music on them and sending them out to people is easy. We need to get across what a great proposition that is, and how that makes us different.'

When it comes to assessing the competition, organizations need to understand what it is that differentiates them from other companies. Schmidt believes that in the case of Peoplesound, it's the unique content that the company has in the form of the music that appears on its site.

'On the internet, you need to have differentiated content. Someone like AOL, for instance, needs to be more like a narrowcast broadcast organization. It needs to recognize that what it has, particularly since its acquisition of Time Warner, is unique content.

'We need to focus on the thing that makes us unique, which is content. Often the problem with dotcom businesses is a lack of focus. People approach us to put music on their sites, and I think: why? You'll notice that there isn't any music news on our site. That's because other sites do that well. Why would we try to do it? It's not why people come to us.'

For Brent Hoberman, co-founder of lastminute.com, assessing the competitive landscape and his company's position in it is tough. 'It's very difficult to benchmark performance,' he says. 'You can only really do it against public companies that have published their figures.'

It's not immediately obvious who lastminute's

competitors are. It's tempting to see travel agents as its main competition. But lastminute sells a lot of products that have nothing to do with travel, and besides, it's not really where someone would look if they were planning a holiday in six months' time. Hoberman sees his company as an entirely new form of intermediary, which competes for market share with a huge range of companies, but also partners with those companies wherever possible.

'Is the web just about disintermediation?' he muses. 'When I wrote the business plan for lastminute, I thought the web was entirely about that, and I found myself thinking that I must be mad for coming up with this idea for a company that was, essentially, an intermediary. But people need intermediaries. I'm not going to go to HarperCollins for a book. So you have Amazon, which is an intermediary. Not that many people think: "I want a First Choice holiday" or "I want a Thomson holiday". They just want the widest choice of available holidays. That's why we partner everywhere. Our view is to be friendly with as many people as possible.'

The big holiday companies know that people want a wide choice of holiday options – it's why some of them also own travel agents. Lastminute is reliant on suppliers like the tour operators to sell items through the site, so those tour operators are often partnering with a company that their own travel agency businesses compete with. They're prepared to do so because lastminute can sell their holiday cheaper than they can get away with. If a tour operator has a holiday unsold, it's better to sell it at a very low price, even one that means it loses money, than not sell it at all, which means that it loses a lot more money. But that tour operator doesn't want to sell its holidays dirt cheap itself, because then people will be discouraged from ever paying the full price.

Enter lastminute, which can sell the holiday unbranded, and therefore cheaper. As mentioned earlier, that doesn't mean price alone is a good point of differentiation for lastminute. The challenge for lastminute is to define itself against the competition by stressing what's unique about it. That means pushing the tens of thousands of items it has on sale through its thousand-odd relationships with suppliers, each one of them individually and separately negotiated. It means getting away from the perception that it is a travel retailer – travel makes up 60 per cent of its revenues, split roughly equally between flights, hotels and packages. And it means getting away from the perception that it's just cheap (often it isn't, particularly), and focusing on the site being the best place to go for people who want to treat themselves.

Jungle.com has had to accommodate constant changes in the competitive landscape into the way it does business. All the product categories it specializes in are e-commerce classics: computer-related goods, CDs, games and videos are all among the biggest sellers online. That means that new competitors are springing up all the time. In the company's core market of computer peripherals and software, the main competition offline was PC World in the consumer market and Action Direct in the business market. On the web, it is companies like dabs.com and buy.com.

Although it deals in items that are sold widely online, managing director Steve Bennett sees jungle's heritage as the thing that will set it apart from its numerous competitors. 'Anyone can become an internet retailer, but to sell something like computer products online, you have to know the computer industry. That probably means you're already in retail or mail order, and to go from retail or mail order onto the web takes a lot of balls.'

The nature of jungle's relationships with other businesses keeps on changing. In part, this is because the internet has opened up new revenue streams for the company. For example, it now finds itself taking advertising on the site. This is novel for a business based around retailing. The types of advertising vary, as do the commercial relationships behind them. A company like mobile phone retailer Carphone Warehouse, for example, has a presence within the 'friends of the jungle' section of the site, which means that jungle customers are sent to Carphone Warehouse's site as jungle's preferred supplier of mobile phones. In return, jungle has a similar presence on the Carphone Warehouse site. Confectionery company Thorntons, on the other hand, has a commission deal – it pays a certain amount to jungle for every customer passed on by the site. Other advertisers simply pay a set fee to appear on jungle. Software Warehouse was never a media property, and these kinds of revenues are by no means central to what jungle.com does. But they are an interesting example of a company finding itself in commercial relationships with organizations it would otherwise have been very unlikely to have anything to do with.

It is also an interesting exercise in trying to assess who is and who isn't a competitor. As discussed in Chapter 5, the internet tends by its nature to stretch brands, and retailers often end up selling items they would never have dreamt of selling offline. Internet companies have traditionally tried to widen their focus as they've grown, moving from selling one product category to selling many. Having built up trust and retail credibility, the reasoning goes, why not use that to sell a broader range of products? The goal is to create an overarching internet retail brand that is at the front of people's minds when they think about buying anything online, or indeed of buying anything. Software Warehouse, as the name suggests, was focused on selling software. Jungle.com, as well as computer-related products such as software and peripherals, also sells entertainment products. Amazon.com started off as an online bookshop, but it now also sells everything from health and beauty products to toys and kitchenware. It even hosts auctions, acquiring a stake in centuries-old auctioneer Sotheby's in June 1999.

That poses some interesting questions when it comes to the kind of advertising and reciprocal promotional relationships a company like jungle.com now finds itself entering into. Because if a brand is expanding to take in new types of product, and other companies do the same, its range of competitors can only grow. Originally, for example, Amazon was one of the commercial partners with a presence in 'friends of the jungle'. Jungle soon realized, however, that with both companies' ever-expanding range of product categories, they were in pretty much direct competition. The deal was swiftly terminated.

The internet introduces new types of supplier that businesses will have to deal with. Technology is at the heart of making an internet presence tick, and so IT departments will have to talk to new types of technology vendor. More crucially, companies have to make a decision about their attitude towards internet service companies, agencies, consultancies, or whatever you want to call them. Some companies prefer to conceive, plan and build their entire internet presence in-house, which is a perfectly reasonable route to go down. But in order to pull it off, that company will need to devote considerable resources to it, and employ people who understand every phase of the web development process. The supplier landscape is a crowded one. There are various services a company might want to buy in, and various types of supplier offering them. Which type of organization a company chooses to use, if any, the nature of its relationship with them, and the amount it pays, will vary. The following is just a snapshot of some of the options, and the examples are just the very tip of a very large iceberg.

There are business strategy and consultancy companies; as well as the traditional strategic management consultancies, there are others that specifically focus on the internet. There are suppliers with a technology bias, ranging from traditional IT services players, through technology consultancies, to technology specialists that specialize in internet development. There are companies with an expertise in design, in the creation of usable interfaces, in so-called information architecture. As in the offline world, there are companies with a narrower business focus, for example on brand development, or marketing. There are companies that do more than one of the above, including several that claim to be able to do all of them. Unsurprisingly, a lot of those in the last category are American.

This last group are an interesting development. In the early days of the web, most businesses, if they had a web presence, employed a single supplier to create it for them. These were usually companies from a design or technical background, along with some agencies from the traditional advertising and marketing industries. As the market grew, the independent digital agencies moved into offering a larger and larger range of services. As the size of budgets grew, along with the importance of internet development to businesses, so clients became increasingly willing to use multiple suppliers for multiple jobs, just like they would in the real world: one company for business strategy, another for design, another for technology, and so on. Those suppliers frequently work in tandem, sometimes with one project managing others.

The mega-suppliers are interesting because they're trying to bring back all responsibility for a company's web presence into a single pair of hands. This isn't the norm in other areas of business. You wouldn't catch a management consultancy actually implementing its recommendations, nor would an advertising agency shoot a commercial it had come up with.

The supplier market is a confusing one for clients. It all depends on the size of the client, the scope of its ambitions, and the confidence it has to do work itself. Most companies will want to do at least some of the business thinking behind an internet project themselves – they're the ones that know their own business best. But very few will go through the whole process, from conception to construction, without using some kind of external supplier.

*

Businesses are at least partly defined by their positioning within a complex web of interrelationships with other organizations, whether they be competitors or companies they have business relationships with. Just as the internet can shake up the internal processes and the business focus of every company, so it can profoundly alter that positioning.

It spawns new competitors, takes companies into areas they have never previously dreamed of occupying; it makes competitors co-operate with each other; and introduces new kinds of suppliers into the equation. The trick is to be nimble, to understand how those relationships are changing, and adapt accordingly. Companies need to react to potential competitive threats before they become threatening. They need to avoid too blinkered a focus on the present and take a calm view of what the future will hold. And they need to understand that if they're not alive to the threat posed by new competitors, they'll be eaten before they realize it.

CHAPTER SEVEN

CONCLUSION

For the majority of this book, it must have sounded like I have a downer on dotcoms. I haven't. For the most part, they are truly vibrant and exciting new businesses that are shaking up the business world. They are a phenomenal catalyst for change. They are forcing businesses and markets into areas they never dreamed they'd go. Some of them will become the biggest businesses. But most won't. Most start-ups of the last five years won't exist in another five. For all the problems established businesses have in coming to terms with the internet and how it affects them, there are certain key advantages they enjoy. That doesn't mean all traditional businesses will flourish online. Being established, having a brand, knowing a market, having a customer base, having business relationships in place, all these are hugely valuable, but they don't guarantee success, any more than being a nimble-footed dotcom does. They still need to be visionary, they still need to grasp the opportunities, and they still need to think long-term about the future of their business.

Yes, dotcoms will tend to be more adaptable than

established businesses. They can get to market quickly, invest at higher levels and with more risk than most traditional businesses would countenance, and they have the flexibility to change what they do completely, should market conditions demand it. That also means that they don't have any firm business processes, ways of doing business that they know work. They're having to improvise, change, feel their way forward. The ability to change, however, can work against them, making it difficult for them to keep a lid on their growth and keep functioning as a unit. If everything changes, no one knows what to do next. Established companies, on the other hand, have processes in place; they know how to do business.

Similarly, it's true that new companies can exploit the gaps in a market no one knew were there. Online business-to-business trading exchanges allow a multiplicity of organizations to communicate and trade with each other in a way that would never have been possible before; they'd have had to conduct each conversation and each transaction individually. That exposes weaker suppliers, making the comparison between them and their stronger competitors more obvious. A web site that allows house hunters to search across a database of properties across the country could endanger the business of estate agents, or possibly of printed classified property advertising in newspapers and magazines. In both examples, a new kind of efficiency has been introduced which threatens established players. The other side of this is that established players already have relationships with their customers, whether they be consumers or other businesses. The good ones will understand where they add value, what benefit using their product or service gives their customers. If what they offer is perceived to be valuable, they won't get cut out.

And supposedly smart internet companies aren't invulnerable to being cut out of the equation. If they can do it, so can other people, particularly if what they do is something like a brokerage service based on little more than a piece of software. Their value is in what they do; what's to stop an incumbent doing the same? In most cases, incumbents have a brand that already means something to people; they could be the ones in the best position to exploit these new business efficiencies.

It is undoubtedly the case that dotcoms can raise a lot of money and be valued way beyond the revenue they make. But that's a double-edged sword. The market won't be fooled for long. If a company doesn't make a profit, it won't carry on being valued highly. Announcing a recent set of financial results, when his company lost $317.2 million on sales of just $577.9 million in a quarter, amazon.com founder Jeff Bezos recently joked that the company should be renamed amazon.org, because it's clearly a non-profit-making organization. Cute, yes, but also worrying. Even the most lauded of internet-spawned businesses has been unable to generate the sort of revenue that can prevent it losing money at a frightening rate. At the time of writing, the company had lost $1.5 billion since its birth in 1995, and its share price was languishing at less than a third of the peak it hit at the height of the dotcom boom.

Unsustainably high levels of spending have become the norm among the internet start-ups. Profitability is still a long way off. Compared to this, traditional businesses, with their established revenue streams, understanding of return on investment and knowledge of how to make a profit, don't look in such a bad way after all.

Traditional players can be the ones to benefit from all this, but only if they act quickly and decisively to identify how the internet fits into their business, counter the threats it poses to them, and embrace it as a positive force that can reshape their business for the better.

Some established companies will survive, and some won't. That would have happened anyway; the internet makes it happen quicker. The ones that do survive may find that they change.

There are some new rules, but good business is still good business. When you get down to fundamentals, it's still about finding a group of customers and giving them a product or service which has value for them. It's just the way companies do it that may change. If you're good at what you do, you shouldn't have a problem with that. It's very easy to see the internet dividing the world into incumbents and attackers: the established, old-economy companies with their undoubted experience counterbalanced by their slowness to adapt, against the new dotcoms with their speed to market and flexibility balanced by a short trading history and the inevitable cashflow difficulties. But the real picture isn't as clear-cut as that. Incumbents can themselves be attackers. They can take on the positive characteristics of a dotcom, while benefiting from the experience, expertise, market knowledge, established processes and so on that they have. The clever incumbents will become like attackers, because even though they'll damage their own business by attacking it, they know that in doing so they'll also damage their competitors' businesses. And they realize that if they don't damage their own business, someone else will come along and damage it for them. Charcol Online is a perfect example of this kind of incumbent-attacker.

If established players do start to lose market share to dotcom competitors, all is not lost. An established company may not be first to market, but the advantages it has can enable it to catch up pretty quickly. Buying a dotcom competitor is always an option. For deep-pocketed incumbents, it can be the quickest and simplest way to build a sizeable online presence. Take WHSmith. The company couldn't have afforded to buy amazon.com, but it did buy the largest UK equivalent, a company called the Internet Book Shop, and has since become one of Britain's largest online booksellers.

Be aware that first-mover advantage is just a phrase. It's true for dotcoms that being first is important, but then they need to establish a name from scratch. Being synonymous with a particular market on the internet, as Amazon is with books, is an incalculable advantage. But being first doesn't necessarily mean being best. Rushing to market doesn't always mean victory, particularly if it's done with an incomplete service. An old-economy business can already be synonymous not just with a market on the internet, but with that market full-stop. You may not need to buy into the crazy land-grab. There are plenty of opportunities to catch up. Buying a dotcom is just one of them.

In the final analysis, man cannot live by computing power alone. Within the self-referential universe of the internet, it's easy to forget that whatever technology can achieve, people still need things like food, clothing and shelter. The internet can never change that, at least not until physical matter can be transmitted digitally. And those physical items are still made from scarce commodities that businesses can control. Certain industries are entirely revolutionized by the internet. Others are modified to a far lesser extent. If a company makes a physical object, it can't be replaced by the internet. It's something unique that the old economy has and an area where the new economy is always going to find it difficult to compete.

So if you do make a physical good, can you sit back, relax and ignore it? Not exactly. Even if you're in a market where the internet seems to have virtually no relevance to what you do, you can't ignore it. Take soft drinks. Just because they can't be delivered online, and no one would want to go to a web site which talks about them, that doesn't mean a company that makes them can ignore the internet. It might be able to foster customer loyalty and reinforce its brand values with an entertaining web site, or a sponsorship of an online property. Or it might be able to buy raw materials more cheaply and efficiently from multiple suppliers using the internet.

To continue the soft drinks example, the marketing director of a very large British drinks company told me at an awards ceremony recently that the internet would have no effect on his business, and that the internet industry was as emptily self-congratulatory as the sales promotion industry during its boom period a few years earlier. Three replies occured to me. One: you seem happy to accept free champagne from the industry you disparage. Two: it would be an odd awards ceremony where people weren't self-congratulatory. And three: if you really believe that the effects of the internet on business will be no bigger than the effects of the sales promotion boom, then I guarantee you won't be in a job in ten years' time.

Whenever I think about the internet (and I do so quite a lot), I always have a nagging doubt that we might all be getting suckered into a kind of cult of novelty, with the internet at its centre – that all this 'greatest change to business since the Industrial Revolution' stuff might turn out to be so much hype. Perhaps it *is* the biggest thing to happen since the Industrial Revolution. Or perhaps it's the biggest thing to happen since, say, the invention of the internal combustion engine. Or perhaps it's only the biggest thing to happen since the last really big thing that happened and everyone got excited about – biotechnology, for example, which must at least rival the internet for the position of top future-shaping technological innovation of our time.

The surest sign that the internet really is as important as everyone says will be when it quickly gets assimilated into the everyday. It will stop being internet business, e-business, cyber-business, or whatever buzzword is in vogue this week, and just become business. The clever business people, those who understand what it is that they do – for them, it'll just become part of their job. They're the ones that have a good chance of making a success of this whole internet thing. The internet is just another way of doing business, albeit one that twists and reshapes some very fundamental economic and cultural assumptions.

Just because something is new, that doesn't necessarily mean it's good, and the fact that the internet is new doesn't necessarily mean everything about it is a force for positive change. The internet is changing everything, and you'll often hear it sold as a great force for societal good, improving the way people communicate and reducing the chances of misunderstanding, isolation, alienation, hatred. That may be true, but in reality it's little more than an attempt to sell as desirable something which is inevitable anyway. Remember that the internet has also been the source of its fair share of moral panics. We've all heard how it allows children to make bombs out of hardcore pornography using recipes passed to them by neo-nazis. Change takes place in a moral vacuum; the internet has its own momentum now, and whether it's a good or a bad thing has become irrelevant. It's just a thing, and if you're in business, you have to deal with it.

When we talk about the internet in the future, we'll mean something very different from what we mean about it now. It will be ubiquitous, mainstream, everyday, and more or less invisible.

What does this mean? Well, for a start, it will spread to devices other than the PC. It's already doing so – internet services on mobile devices are becoming increasingly popular. In certain countries, where PC penetration is low, the internet is already far more about mobile phones than it is about computers. And as interactive TV takes off on the new digital television services, more and more of what have traditionally been linear broadcast media will come to resemble the internet as well. When this colossal information and communication network is available everywhere, it will cease to be something isolated, a web browser that you call up on your computer, and

CONCLUSION

become the ubiquitous way you do everything in your life.

The spread of the internet may go beyond the obvious devices: PCs, TVs, mobile phones and so on. At the risk of making myself a hostage to fortune and looking silly when what I predict totally fails to come to fruition, it could appear on kitchen devices like fridges, ovens or even bins. So when someone uses a product or throws it away, the device can order a replacement for them.

The internet will also become a lot faster, and a lot more reliable. People don't tolerate slowness, mistakes, failure or downtime on devices like television in the same way as they do with their already notoriously unreliable computers. TV works, and people will expect the internet on TV to work, and to be as fast as they need it to be. If the internet does become a ubiquitous way of communicating, people will require it to think and act at the same speed as they do.

Broadband services like ADSL and its successors will ensure that this happens, and will profoundly change the way in which people interact with the internet. It will make it easier to move from one place to another speedily, which could be bad news for certain time-saving services like companion engines, whose value is predicated on the current slowness of the net. People will expect to be able to get to wherever they want to be very quickly.

That will all have a profound effect on the way in which businesses use the internet, or whatever we call it then, to talk to their customers. It won't be a case of using a web site to communicate with customers and transact any more – that activity will take place as part of something bigger – as a linked, always-on, interactive interface with customers. When this starts to happen, businesses won't really have a choice whether or not to engage with the internet any more. If they don't, they'll become invisible.

The internet is profoundly democratic in the way it allows people to communicate. Any individual can talk to millions of people across the world, on demand, at any time, and swap experiences. They can compare what different companies are offering them. It can become part of the fabric of their lives, the first place they turn to when they want something. It's about much more than just web sites – it's about services, delivered through the internet, that have a profound effect on the ways in which people conduct their lives.

Traditional businesses often have the advantage that they control commodities, that they have something physical that can't be replicated. The internet alters the balance of power because it introduces new resources that can't be controlled by anyone. And so it looks suspiciously like any company can now do anything. Just as the internet is turning around the way individual businesses operate, so it's having an effect on a macro scale. It's much easier to get a piece of the action, hence the entrepreneurial explosion – one of the big barriers to entry is gone. Companies become differentiated more by the service that they give their customers than by any product they control. As mentioned earlier in this chapter, this is not the whole story, though. If you don't already mine diamonds, you can't suddenly start doing so because of the internet. If you don't already sell clothes, then OK, you might be able to start doing so because of the internet, but you're going to find it an awful lot harder to do so than a company that already sold clothes before the internet existed.

Not every company will need to change what it does from head to toe. Some will; others will have to tweak certain elements of what they do. In the most extreme cases, the internet will force companies to completely re-invent themselves, and alter everything they do. You may not just have to re-engineer some of your business processes: you may have to destroy your business and build a new one. Equally, you may not have to. But you should at least think about whether you need to. The business landscape shifts all the time, and individual businesses change with it. Those businesses constantly need to be reassessing themselves. The internet dramatically speeds the pace of change and means that they have to reassess themselves more often than they've ever had to before, and implement changes more quickly than they've ever had to before.

As I said at the very start of this book, if you're not thinking about how your business is changing, you can be damn sure that your competitors are. The only thing that's certain about the future of business is this: companies that bury their heads in the ground, and hope that the internet will just go away, are sure to fail.

INDEX

Abacus Direct 92
Abbey National 129
acquisition cost of
customers 87–88
Action Direct 216
Adaptability
of Britannica 49–50
of dotcoms 222–223
vision required for
48–50
ADSL (asymmetric digital
subscriber lines) 70,
230
advertising
see also brand
development;
marketing
of bad products
188–189, 204
balance required
170–171

blanket blitz of
190–191
challenges for Charcol
Online 158–159
creative treatment in
186–187
driving responses
155
effectiveness of
161–163, 201–203
internet as medium
199–201
key for britannica.com
44
puns and 'fun' 188
replacement for paid
content 44–54
TV 159
agency recruitment
155–156, 163
AltaVista 45

amazon.com
  BOL comparison with
    183–185
  brand extension
    197–198
  execution, decisiveness
    of 71
  going public, excitement
    at xvi
  intermediary status of
    215
  jungle.com, friendship
    with (and termination
    of) 218
  market,
    synonymousness with
    226
  stocks and logistics
    72–73
  traditional competitors
    and the pace of
    online change 101
  web site usability 68–69
ambitious plans
  of Britannica 52–53
  of Charcol Online
    17–18
AOL 45, 186, 188, 214
ARPANET (Advanced
  Research Projects
  Agency Network) x,
  xiii
attraction of staff
  102–106, 130–131

automated customer
  service software
    82–84

Barnes&Noble.com 71,
  101
BBC 59
Bennett, Steve (jungle.com)
  on advertising
    effectiveness
    161–163, 201–203
  on automated response
    software 82
  consumers, businesses
    and online buying
    66–67
  customer service, labour
    intensive nature of
    79–80
  customer service, mass
    underestimation of
    80–81
  direct selling, rationale
    for 7–9
  domain name,
    difficulties with
    174–75
  product knowledge,
    importance of
    heritage of 217
  staff motivation 132
  staff recruitment, broad
    experience sought
    112–113

trade press, cost-
effectiveness as
advertising media
157
Bezos, Jeff (amazon.com)
224
Blackwell Information
Services 131
bokus.com 193
BOL 71, 183–185
boo.com
brand creation,
difficulties with
154–155
classic example of
control loss 142–144
expectation, reality and
108–109
first-mover, problems of
143–144
generously funded but
bust 57
investor confidence
shaken 137–138
management failure,
scaling for growth
108
marketing budget of
165–166
online brand creation
189–190
PR overkill 192–194
profligacy of 106–109,
144

staff, overpayment of
106–107
technology costs
142–143
Boston Consulting 87
Bradford & Bingley 13
brand development
see also advertising;
marketing
advertising and
153–155, 161–163,
182–183, 200–201
boo.com, difficulties
with 154–155
brand extension by
amazon.com
197–198
brand extension
through jungle.com
197
dotcoms, problems for
57
price and 181
brands
Britannica, strength and
instinctive trust
48–49
differentiation of
178–190
heritage issues 172,
175
internet names and
171–178
key selling points 182

M&S, strength of 32–33
physical dimensions, advantage of 187–188
power of 46
price and staying power of 181
protection of 33–34
stretching of 196–198
value in 49
Branson, Sir Richard 196
Bright Station 143
Britannica
adaptation to change 49–50
ambitiousness of plans 52–53
brand, value in 49
britannica.co.uk, ditching of 54–55
CDs, focus on 41–42
challenge of finding the right people 110–111
change at every level in 51–52
competitive changes for 210
content, editorial policy and 41–42
cultural change in 111
digital media, effect on 40
dotcommed from top-to-toe 53
educational focus 52–53
Encarta and 40–41
future for 56
knowledge repository 48–52
personnel shake-up in 109–111
radical turn-around of 45–46
revenue streams, identification of new 43–44
sales force lay-off 39–44
venarable traditons of 40
vision of 50
web, knowledge revolution and 42–43
what are we to make of it? 55–56
britannica.com
advertising a key for 44
brand strength and instinctive trust 48–49
britannica.co.uk and 45–47
content development 47
global infrastructure of 47

launch ditched 54–55
online media scene overcrowded in UK 53
positioning close to internet giants 44–45
revenue streams, identification of 43–44
vision and speed of adaptation 49–50
broadcast media view of the internet 22
BT (British Telecommunications) 70, 164–165, 176
business landscape, shift and change of 232
business, offline *see* traditional offline business
business-to-business services 63, 86–87
Butterfields 197

Cahoot 129
Cambridge 125
Caprice, Le 213
Carphone Warehouse 217
cashflow problems of dotcoms 146
CDNOW 58, 138, 153
channel conflict
 avoidance of (M&S) 34
cross-channel activities and 31–32
retail vs internet 7–8
Charcol Online
see also John Charcol
advertising challenges for 158–159
aggressive use of internet 14
ambitious plans of 17–18
automated customer service software and 83
business surge 14–15
competitive pressures on 207–210
complaints, escalation procedure for 84
customer base, expansion of 16
customer contact and 89
customers serving themselves 65–66
funding for 150
growth management 125–126
as incumbent attacker 226
launch of 13–14
product lines, traditional separate from online 15–16

INDEX

staff recruitment 105
staff recruitment for
114–115
Chase DeVere 207
Clerkenwell 125
Clickmango 138
Co-operative Bank 129
Colas, Frederic (ex P&G)
interactive marketing in
action 20–29
mobility of labour
121–122
reflect.com, rationale for
147
staff losses to dotcoms
119
collaborative filtering 94
communication with
customers, proactive
89–90
comparison, infinite
possibilities for
61–62, 180
competition
business
interrelationships and
221
competitive vigilance
207
continual reassessment
of 213
defining 213, 214–216
expansion through
211–212

identification of 218
landscape of, constant
change in 210,
216–218
pressures of 207–210
computer direct vendor
(Dell) 5–7, 12,
68–69, 85–86,
116–118, 160
consumer multinational,
adapting to the
internet 18–30,
62–63, 118–119,
146–148
Consumers Association 81
CorporateDirect 66
cultural fit, importance of
99, 123
customer acquisitions, cost
of 87–88
customer service
flexibility the key 85–86
intelligent software for
80
labour intensive nature
of 79–80
online with jungle.com
78–81
online standard
generally dreadful
67–68
perfection before
promotion, policy of
169–171

technology and costs 85
underestimation of
needs 80–81
customers
acquisition, cost of
87–88
communication with,
future of 230–231
compaints procedures
78–82
contact with, Charcol
Online 89
data on, care in use of
92
empowerment by
dotcoms 20, 24, 62
expansion of base 16,
35–37, 64–66
focus on existing 37
fulfilment, a problem
area 72–77
identification a key 35,
63–64
inertia of 87–88
interaction with
vendors, changing
nature of 59, 61–63,
83–84, 89
intolerance of failure
77–78
labour-intensiveness of
serving 79–80
one-to-one
communication with

93–94
online, differing from
traditional 65–66
primacy of 60–62,
94–95
proactive
communication with
89–90
retention of 88–89
serving themselves,
Charcol Online
65–66
targeting messages to
92–93
technology and service
of 82–85
Tesco online, profiles of
35–36
value in existing
customer bases
223–224

Daimler-Chrysler
206–207
Data Protection Act 92
delivery of orders, problem
area 73–77
Dell Computer
customer service,
flexibility the key
85–86
marketing, effectiveness
of traditional
methods 160

product configuration,
    customer choice and
    12
staff motivation
    problems 116–118
transferring business
    online 5–7
web site usability
    68–69
democracy of the internet
    231
development of the
    internet xiii-xv
digitally transmittable
    products, advantages
    for 58
direct selling, rationale for
    007–9
Dixons Stores Group
    119–120, 146
domain name difficulties
    174–76
dormusic.com 64
dotcoms
    see also internet; online
        services
    adaptability of 222–223
    attraction of
        entrepreneurial staff
        130–131
    'blank sheet of paper'
        status of 4
    brand establishment
        problems for 57

cashflow problems of
    146
catalysts for change 222
customer empowerment
    by 62
ethos of 100–101
flexibility and change,
    advantages in 3
funding a minefield for
    144–145
gap exploitation 223
high risk businesses 135
hyper-growth, challenge
    of 101–102, 123–130
little to lose 33
offline competitors,
    dealing with
    225–226
profits doubts 224–225
shakeout of 57–58
spending and funding,
    high rates of
    135–142
DoubleClick 92
down-sizing at Britannica
    109–111
Drkoop 58, 138
Dunn & Bradstreet/AC
    Nielsen 131

EasyEverything 10
EasyGroup 10
EasyJet 9–12, 171
eBay 28, 72, 169, 197

e-commerce volumes at
    M&S 33
Economist 47
economy of the internet
    based on confidence 45
    infinite nature of 61
Edinburgh 125
educational focus of
    Britannica 52–53
egg 123, 129, 172–173,
    208
E-INSIGHT 141
E-LOAN 207, 208
e-mail, intrusiveness of 91
Empire Stores 113
Encarta and Britannica
    40–41
Encyclopaedia Britannica
    see Britannica
entrepreneurial visionaries
    131–132
e*trade 101
Excite 27, 45, 46, 210
expectation and reality
    (boo.com) 108–109
experiences of the internet
    see internet
    engagement

failure, customers'
    intolerance of 77–78
First Choice Holidays 215
first mover considerations
    143–144, 153, 206,
    226
First Tuesday xiv
Ford 175, 206–207
foreign languages,
    accommodation to
    51–52
Freeserve xiii, 119–120,
    146, 165, 186–188
fulfilment of customer
    demand, a problem
    area 72–77
functional boundaries,
    blurring of 96–97
funding
    see also investment
    boo.com and 142–144
    Charcol Online and
    150
    dilemma for traditional
    business 145, 149
    difficulties for traditional
    businesses 2
    dotcom minefield
    144–145
    high-tech, US culture of
    58
    internet start-up market
    139–140
    investor confidence and
    137–138
    investor types 139–140
    online services 139–142
    P&G seeking alternative
    external 146–148

INDEX

profits distantly forecast
137
spending and, high rates
of 135–142
Strauss on 150

gap exploitation 223
General Motors 206–207
generic domain names
178
geographical frontiers,
non-existence of 56
geographical monopolies
of traditional business
58
global infrastructure of
britannica.com 47
grey-haired experience
112–113
growth, management of
108, 125–128
see also hyper-growth
Guardian Unlimited 47

Hall, Chris (Dell
Computers) 6,
85–86, 117–118, 160
HarperCollins 215
high-tech funding, US
culture of 58
HMV 214
Hoberman, Brent
(lastminute.com)
aggressive PR

promotion of 195
competition, difficulties
in defining 214–216
flexibility and change,
dotcom advantages in
3
on marketing spend
167
on price and brand
staying power 181
staff, retention of 122
on start-up spending
136
traditional business and
monopoly on
geography 58
human resources *see* staff
hyper-growth
see also growth,
management of
challenge of 101–102,
123–130, 124–125
dangers of 149

ICANN (Internet
Corporation for
Assigned Names and
Numbers) 178
Iceland 36–37
iCrunch 213, 214
incumbent attacker,
Charcol Online 226
Industrial Revolution xi,
xii, 228

inertia
of customers 87–88
of traditional business 1
integration
cross-channel policy of
31–32
of new staff 129–130
offline with online
operations 76
of online services
119–121
staffing and 120–121
web presence fit and
31–32, 34–35
Intel 23
interaction customers-
vendors, changing
nature of 59, 61–63,
89
interactive marketing
20–29
intermediaries changing
role of 16–17
intermediary status of
amazon.com 215
internal movement of staff
113–116
international direct-selling
38
internet
see also dotcoms; online
selling
adapting to the
ramifications of the

18–30
blurring of functional
boundaries by the
96–97
broadcast media view of
the 22
change and speed of the
xv-xvii
comparison, infinite
possibilities for on the
61–62, 180
customer base
expansion through
35–37
customer
communication,
future of 230–231
customer in charge on
the 20, 24
democracy, profound,
of the 231
development of the xiii-
xv
economy based on
confidence 45
economy, infinite nature
of 61
exacerbation of human
resources issues
133–134
geographical frontiers,
non-existence of
56
goldrush talk 135

hype concerning the ix-x

interaction, customer-vendor, changes brought about by the 59, 61–63, 89

macro scale effects of the 231–232

magnification of people issues by the 96–97

moral panic, as source of 229

origins x-xiii

positive force for traditional business 225–226

relevance for all 227–228

reliability and speed improvements 230

staff recruitment problems 3

start-up market 139–140

threat, apparent, of the 12–13

traditional needs and the 226–227

ubiquitous, invisible future of the 228–231

youth of the 39

Internet Book Shop 226

internet engagement

amazon.com xvi, 68–69, 71–73, 101, 183–185, 197–198, 215, 218, 226

boo.com 57, 106–109, 137–138, 142–144, 154–155, 165–166, 189–190, 192–194

Britannica 39–56, 109–111, 210

Dell Computers 5–7, 12, 68–69, 85–86, 116–118, 160

EasyJet 9–12

Iceland Stores 36–37

John Charcol 12–18, 65–66, 83–84, 89, 105, 114–116, 125–127, 150, 158–159, 207–210, 226

lastminute.com xvi, 11, 58, 69, 113, 122, 136, 167, 181, 214–216

Marks & Spencer 29–35, 37–39, 76–77, 82, 85, 120–121, 149, 169–171, 175–176, 211–212

peoplesound.com 59, 100–101, 105–106, 131–132, 136, 182–183, 200–201, 213, 214

Software Warehouse/jungle.com 7–9, 66–67, 78–82, 112, 132–133, 157, 161–163, 174–175, 201–203, 216–218
Tesco Stores 35–37
Procter & Gamble 18–30, 62–63, 118–119, 146–148
internet-only companies *see* dotcoms
investment *see* funding
Jackson, Tim (QXL) 131
John Charcol (mortgage broker)
  see also Charcol Online
  advertising challenges for 158–159
  aggressive embrace of internet 14
  change, agent of 17
  customer base, differences in online 65–66
  customer service interactions, opportunities and 83–84
  expansion of customer base 16
  internet threat to 12–13
  market leadership of 207

online developments of 13–16
product lines, online separate from traditional 15–16
radical choices of 13–14
staff transfers within 114–116
supplier contact 209
Jones, Bob (jungle.com) 113
jungle.com
  see also Software Warehouse
  advertising effectiveness, research on 201–203
  brand development, direct advertising and 161–163
  competitive landscape, constant change in 216–218
  customer service online 78–81
  customer service, launch swamping of 80–81
  customer service, use of intelligent software in 80
  different online businesses of 66–67
  domain name,

INDEX

difficulties with 174–175

labour-intensive costs of customer service 79

mission statement and core values of 132–133

product choice for online sales 7

staff recruitment, broad experience sought 112

trade press, cost-effectiveness as advertising media 157

JungleDirect 66

Jupiter Communications 63

knowledge vendor, rollercoaster ride of Britannica 39–56, 109–111, 210

KPMG 143

labour-intensiveness of customer service 79–80

Ladbroke's 176

Lane Fox, Martha xvi, 122, 167, 194–5

lastminute.com
brand development and price 181

competition, difficulties in defining 214–216

marketing spend and 167

media, saturation coverage of xvi

non-executive directors, experience of 113

PR overkill 194–196

site navigation 69

stakeholding policy of 122

start-up spending 136

thought process informing usage 11

traditional business, advantages of 58

letsbuyit.com 28

Levine, Mike (peoplesound.com) 101

logistics
amazon.com stocks and 72–73

problem areas 73–77

Tesco experience 75

London, City of 126–127

Loot 139

Lubbock, Victoria (Recruit Media) 102, 103

Lycos 210

McDonalds 213

McKinsey 99, 119
macro-scale effects of the internet 231–232
Marconi Corporation 86
marketing
  see also advertising; brand development
  brand expansion and 218–219
  centrality of 19
  free offers 185
  grass roots basis of eBay 167–168
  market research 213
  scatter-gun approach to 157
  spending on 159–160, 165–167
  stance of peoplesound.com 182–183
  synonymousness of amazon.com 226
  traditional methods, effectiveness of 160
  waste by internet companies 164, 166–167
Marks & Spencer
  automated response software, customer service and 82
  brand, protection of 33–34
  brand, strength of 32–33
  channel conflict, avoidance of 34
  competition and 211–212
  customer service, technology and costs 85
  domain name, difficulties with 175–176
  existing customer focus 37
  frustration source for e-commerce operators 31
  improvement, limitless possibilities for 149
  integration, web presence fit 31–32, 34–35
  international direct-selling 38
  internet integration, staffing and 120–121
  service perfection before promotion, policy of 169–171
  stores as distribution centres 76
  troubled retailer 29–30
media overcrowding 53–54
Microsoft 40–42, 50, 210

Miller Freeman 63
mobility of labour
   121–122
money *see* funding
MoneyExtra 207
MoneySupermarket
   207
mortgage broking, internet
   and innovation (John
   Charcol) 12–18,
   65–66, 83–84, 89,
   105, 114–116,
   125–127, 150,
   158–159, 207–210,
   226
motivation of staff 50,
   116–118, 128–129,
   132–133
MP3.com 213, 214
MSN 45
Mullins, Aimee 187
Music Week 64
musicunsigned.com 213
myhome.com 26

names *see* domain names
Netmortgage 207
New Statesman 47
Newsnight (BBC) 195
Newsweek 47
Nielsen, AC, MMS 161,
   164
non-executive directors,
   role of 113

office space, price inflation
   of 125–126
offline business *see*
   traditional offline
   business
Omidyar, Pierre (eBay)
   169
One in a Million 176
one-to-one communication
   with customers
   93–94
online services
   see also dotcoms;
   internet
   complaints 78–82
   customer group
      identification a key
      35
   developments of John
      Charcol 13–16
   flexibility a key
      85–86
   fulfilment a problem
      area 72–77
   funding of 139–142
   improvement, limitless
      scope for 149–150
   international expansion
      through 38
   intolerance of failure of
      77–78
   intrusiveness of e-mail
      91
   media scene

overcrowded in UK 53–54
separation from traditional business 15–16
separation or integration of 119–121
standard generally dreadful 67–68
organization structure, rigity and problems 20
origins of the internet x-xiii

P&G Interactive 23, 24, 25
passing off domain names 176–177
PC World 216
peoplesound. com
  market research, assessing competition 213
  brand development and online advertising 200–201
  customer-retailer interaction and 59
  dotcom ethos 100–101
  marketing stance of 182–183
  staff recruitment 105–106
  start-up spending 136
  starting-up vs day-to-day management 131–132
  uniqueness, focus on 214
personalization and choice 94
perspective, the need for 4–5
Plent, Jason (Britannica)
  adaptation, vision and speed of change 48–50
  advertising, replacement for paid content 44–54
  belief in his business 41–42
  brand, power of 46
  britannica.co.uk, ditching of 54–55
  bullishness about future 45–47, 53–54
  challenge of finding the right people 110–111
  on competitive changes 210
  confidence of 45
  content development 47, 52–53
  content, editorial policy

and 41–42
down-sizing 109–111
on search engines 47–48
staff motivation, a challenge 50
prices, competition on 179–181
primacy of customers 60, 61–62, 94–95
prioritizing, difficulties in 149
proactive communications 89–90
Procter & Gamble (P&G)
customer power and 62–63
funding, seeking alternative external 146–148
internet, adapting to the 18–30
staff recruitment problems 118–119
products
choice for online sales 7
configuration of, customer choice and 12
knowledge of, importance of heritage of 217
online separate from traditional 15–16
profits
demonstrating a path to 151
distantly forecast 137
doubts with dotcoms 224–225
profligacy of boo.com 106–109, 144
Prudential Insurance 123, 129, 172–173
public relations, overkill by 192–196

Question Time (BBC) 195
QXL 28, 131

Recruit Media 102
recruitment of staff 3, 105–106, 112–115, 118–119
reflect.com 25, 27, 147–148
relationship marketing 25–27
relevance of internet for all 227–228
reliability and speed of the internet 230
retail giant, internet strategy of M&S 29–35, 37–39, 76–77, 82, 85, 120–121, 149, 169–171, 175–176, 211–212

retail vs internet, channel conflict 7–8
retention of
 customers 88–89
 staff 103, 121–123
revenue streams, identification of 43–44, 54
Revolution xv, 54, 67, 102, 177, 188
Robinson, Anne 81
Robinson, Peter (M&S)
 on advertising balance 170–171
 on automated response software 82
 on competition 211–212
 customer service, technology and costs 85
 e-commerce volumes 33
 focus on existing customers 37
 fringe vs core activities 33
 importance of web presence fit 30–39
 integration, offline with online operations 76
 internet as focus of overseas expansion 38
 internet integration, staffing and 120–121
 online presence, on purpose of 35
 prioritizing, difficulties of 149
 stores, advantages of 34–35
 waking the sleeping giants 38–39
Rose, Jim (QXL) 131

Saatchi & Saatchi 198
Sainsbury 176
Saville's 207, 208
Schmidt, Ernesto (peoplesound.com)
 on brand building and advertising 182–183, 200–201
 competition, definition against 213
 on customer-retailer interaction 59
 established companies, traditional ailments of 100
 on market research 213
 on staff recruitment 105–106
 on start-up spending 136
 starting-up vs day-to-

day management
131–132

uniqueness, focus on
214

Screentrade 17

search-engines 47–48

separation of online
services 15–16,
119–121

Shopsmart 17

Shoreditch 125

Silicon Valley 130

smile 129

Software Warehouse
see also jungle.com
brand extension
through jungle.com
197
direct selling, rationale
for 7–9
jungle.com, competitive
relationship with
217–218
retail, mail-order focus
of 78
staff motivation 132
staff recruitment, broad
experience sought
112

software, online natural
(jungle.com) 7–9,
66–67, 78–82, 112,
132–133, 157,
161–163, 174–175,

201–203, 216–218

Soho 111

Sotheby's 197, 218

spin-off creation,
advantages of 123,
129

staff
attraction of 102–106,
130–131
boo.com and
106–109
Britannica and
109–111
cultural fit, importance
of 99, 123
Dell and 116–118
exacerbation of human
resources issues
133–134
experience deficit in
98–99
finding the right people
98
grey-haired experience
112–113
growth and human
issues 127–128
integration of new
129–130
internal movement of
113–116
John Charcol and
115–116
losses to dotcoms 119

magnification of people issues 96–97
motivation of 50, 116–118, 128–129, 132–133
P&G and 118–119
recruitment of 3, 105–106, 112–115, 118–119, 123–130
retention of 103, 121–123
stock options, nature and value of 104
wages, hype about 102, 104
stakeholding policy of lastminute.com 122
start-up market 139–140
starting vision vs day-to-day management 131–132
Strauss, Toby (Charcol Online)
 on automated customer service software 83–84
 on competitive vigilance 207
 on funding 150
 managing growth 125–127
 on marketing spend 159–160
 online customers differ from traditional 65–66
 staff recruitment 105
 staff transfers, selectivity and 114–116
 supplier contact, value of the internet for 209–210
 transformation of mortgage broking business 14–16
structural constraints on traditional business 2–3, 99–101
success, ingredients for 59
supplier contact, value of internet for 209–210
swizzle.co.uk 27

technology vending specialisms 219–221
Tesco Stores
 logistics 75
 online customers profiled 35–36
 personal experience of online shopping from 77
 spin-off creation, advantages of 123, 129
Thomson Holidays 215
Thorntons 217

INDEX

Time Warner 214
trade press, cost-
effectiveness as
advertising medium
157
traditional offline business
ailments of 100
commodity control 231
dotcom competitors,
dealing with
225–226
existing business as
hindrance to internet
progress 3–4
funding dilemma for
145, 149
geographical
monopolies of 58
inertia of 1
internet investment,
difficulties for 2
internet, a positive force
for 225–226
structural constraints on
2–3
structural ossification of
99–101
value in existing
customer bases
223–224
vision, need for 222
travel, a high information
product 11

Unilever 19, 26, 27, 62
United Information
Services 131

Virgin 176, 196
visionary entrepreneurs
131–132

wages, hype concerning
102, 104
Washington Post 47
Watchdog (BBC) 81
Waterstones 184
web presence fit,
importance of 30–39
web site
design 68–71
navigation 69
usability 68–69
Webex 188
WH Smith 71, 185, 226
Which Web Trader 81

Yahoo 45, 46, 210